# The Studebaker National Museum...
## Over a Century on Wheels

**Andrew Beckman**
*Archivist, Studebaker National Museum*

**M.T. Publishing Company, Inc.**
P.O. Box 6802
Evansville, Indiana 47719-6802
www.mtpublishing.com

Copyright © 2008
Studebaker National Museum
All rights reserved.

No part of this publication may be translated, reproduced, or transmitted in any form or by any means, electronic or mechanical, including photocopying and recording, or by any information storage and retrieval system, without expressed written permission of the copyright owners and M.T. Publishing Company, Inc.

The materials were compiled and produced using available information. M.T. Publishing Company, Inc., and the Studebaker National Museum regret they cannot assume liability for errors or omissions.

Library of Congress Control Number: 2008929714

ISBN: 978-1-934729-02-1

Graphic Design and Layout by Mary Meehan Firtl
FirtlMind Designs
South Bend, IN 46615

Pre-press work by M.T. Publishing Company, Inc.

Printed in the
United States of America

# The Studebaker National Museum...
## Over a Century on Wheels

*Out of 1,000 Commemorative Edition Copies this book is number* 709.

# TABLE OF CONTENTS

Chapter One: Meet the "Studenbeckers" ................................................................. 5

Chapter Two: Wait for the Wagon ........................................................................... 9

Chapter Three: Transitions ..................................................................................... 25

Chapter Four: Evolution ......................................................................................... 35

Chapter Five: Recovery .......................................................................................... 63

Chapter Six: Duty ................................................................................................... 79

Chapter Seven: Limelight ....................................................................................... 91

Chapter Eight: Decline ......................................................................................... 115

Chapter Nine: Legacy ........................................................................................... 143

Chapter Ten: The Collection ................................................................................ 153

**The Original Studebaker Collection:**
Vehicles listed with this credit were part of the Studebaker Corporation's private collection. The collection was given to the city of South Bend in 1966, and is now part of the Studebaker National Museum.

**Photo credits:**
All images are courtesy of Matt Cashore, the Center for History, Richard Quinn, Charlene Rule, Trevor Ruszkowski and TR22 Photography, and the Studebaker National Museum Archives. The Studebaker National Museum extends sincere thanks to Mr. Cashore, the Center for History, Mr. Quinn, Ms. Rule, and Mr. Ruszkowski for their generous contributions to this book.

**Acknowledgments:**
The Studebaker National Museum would like to acknowledge its many donors and supporters who made this project possible. The Museum owes a sincere debt of gratitude to the many stewards of its collection since its beginnings in the late 19th century. An equal debt is owed to those who have contributed the vehicles and artifacts that comprise the collection. The generosity of these fine individuals has fueled the Studebaker legacy for generations to come. The author would like to thank Studebaker National Museum Trustee Pat Ruszkowski for providing the vision for this project, and the staff at the Studebaker National Museum for their assistance and support. Finally, the author would like to thank the entire Beckman family for immersing him in Studebaker lore from a very early age.

# STUDEBAKER FAMILY TREE

## *John Clement Studebaker (1799 – 1887) married Rebecca Mohler (1802 – 1887)*

### Children:

1. Henry (1821 – 1824)
2. Sally (1822 – 1902) married Philip Welch (1816 – 1895)
3. Jeremiah (1823 – 1824)
4. Nancy (1825 – 1872) married John Lucas (1821 – unknown)
5. Henry (1826 – 1895) married 1st Susan Studybaker (1829 – 1871), married 2nd Prescilla Krieghbaum
6. Delilah (1828 – 1831)
7. Elizabeth (1829 – 1909) married George Witwer (1838 – unknown)
8. Clement (1831 – 1901) married 1st Charity Bratt (1831 – 1863), married 2nd Anna Milburn Harper (1842 – 1916)
9. John Mohler (1833 – 1917) married Mary Jane Stull (1836 – 1921)
10. Peter Everest (1836 – 1897) married 1st Dora Handley (1836 – 1865), married 2nd Alice Woodbury Mitchell (unknown), married 3rd Mary Ewing Gunthie (1831 – 1913)
11. Rebecca (1837 – 1915)
12. Maria (1840 – 1925)
13. Jacob Franklin (1844 – 1887) married Harriet Chord (1848 – 1909)

### Children of Henry and Susan Studybaker:

1. Emma (1853 – 1942) married Amos Bowman (1847 – 1921)
2. Samuel (1854 – 1915) married Mary Martin (1854 – 1938)
3. Laura (1855 – 1876)
4. Edith (1857 – 1942) married Irving Gingrich (1853 – unknown)
5. Lydia (1859 – 1930) married Jack Chillas (1858 – 1940)
6. Clement W. (1861 – 1934) married Mary van den Bosch (1860 – 1928)
7. Adelle (1874 – 1959)
8. William K. (1875 – 1959) married Emilia Hodson (unknown)
9. Peter Everest (1877 – 1959) married Olive Lewis (unknown)
10. Arthur H. (1883 – 1918) married Irene Cronk (unknown)

### Children of Clement and Anna Milburn Harper:

1. George Milburn (1865 – 1939) married Ada Lantz (1866 – 1954)
2. Anne (1868 – 1931) married Charles Arthur Carlisle (1864 – 1938)
3. Clement Jr. (1871 – 1932) married Alice Rhawn (1868 – 1945)

### Children of John Mohler and Mary Jane Stull:

1. Lillie Elgin (1860 – 1901) married Harry Johnson (1852 – 1916)
2. Gracie (1862 - 1946) married Frederick Fish (1852 – 1936)
3. John Mohler II (1871 – 1947) married Lillie Lingle (1879 – 1947)

### Children of Peter Everest and Dora Handley:

1. Wilbur Fisk (1857 – 1905) married Fannie Dulin (1861 – unknown)
2. Mary R. (1860 – 1937) married Nelson J. Riley (1858 – 1916)
3. Dora L. (1860 – unknown) married William R. Innis (1859 – 1920)
4. Etta (1863 – unknown)

### Children of Jacob Franklin and Harriet Chord:

1. Helen (1872 – 1917) married Russel Ulrich (unknown)
2. Ida (1870 – 1934) married 1st Edward Kuhns, married 2nd Rex Sherer  Edward Kuhns (unknown) married 2nd Rex Sherer (unknown)

# Chapter One: Meet the "Studenbeckers"

# Meet the Studenbeckers

In June of 1736, the Dutch ship *Harle* left Frefeld, Germany, destined for Philadelphia. Among its 388 passengers were Peter, Clement, and Henry Studenbecker. The family were sword makers in the old country, and the family line can be traced back to the 11th Century.

In the new world, "Studenbecker" became Studebaker, and the family settled in a religious community in Ephrata, Pennsylvania. Peter Studebaker and Peter Studebaker, Jr., soon opened a blacksmith shop near York, Pennsylvania.

Peter Studebaker's son John Clement opened a blacksmith shop of his own in the Gettysburg-area village of Pinetown, Pennsylvania.

*Rebecca Studebaker*   *John C. Studebaker*

In 1820, John C. Studebaker married Rebecca Mohler, and together raised ten children. John C.'s skills as a blacksmith were unquestioned, but running a profitable business proved difficult. With hopes of better fortunes elsewhere, the family moved west to Ashland, Ohio in 1835.

Another blacksmith shop was opened, but proved no more successful than the first. The elder Studebaker boys toiled in the shop with their father, each learning the blacksmithing and wagon making trade. Long, hard days were the norm as the family labored to settle its debts.

John and Rebecca's oldest daughter Sally and her husband Philip Welch moved to South Bend in the mid 1840s. The new community on the south bend of the St. Joseph River offered substantial opportunities for enterprising young men. Henry and Clement Studebaker joined Mr. and Mrs. Welch in South Bend in 1850, and were soon joined by the rest of the family.

*The Studebaker Brothers: (L-R)*
*Henry, Jacob, Clement, Peter, John M. (J.M.)*

*The east race of the St. Joseph River in downtown South Bend c. 1870.*

*Downtown South Bend c. 1860.*

*From the original Studebaker Collection.*

### 1835 Conestoga Wagon

John C. Studebaker built this Conestoga wagon around 1835 for his family's journey from Pennsylvania to Ohio.

The Conestoga wagon was a very primitive wagon built strictly for cargo. There is no provision for passenger seating, and unlike modern wagons, there are no springs or suspension for cushioning the ride.

Despite claims to the contrary, there is no evidence that H & C Studebaker manufactured Conestoga wagons. By the 1850s, the Conestoga was obsolete, having been replace by the more refined "Prairie Schooner"-style wagons.

Henry Studebaker took work at a blacksmith shop upon his arrival in South Bend, and brother Clement taught school. The brothers, however, sought to open a business of their own. On February 16, 1852, with assets totaling $68 in cash, a set of blacksmith tools and a forge, H & C Studebaker opened its doors on the southwest corner of Michigan and Jefferson streets in downtown South Bend. The first and only customer of the day was a gentleman whose horse needed shoeing. The day's receipts totaled 25 cents.

South Bend was a burgeoning city in the 1850s. Rail service to Toledo, Ohio, arrived in 1851, and the St. Joseph River supplied power and transportation to the Great Lakes. The city boasted nearly 100 manufacturing concerns by 1861, many of them located downtown or on the St. Joseph River.

John Mohler Studebaker considered joining his brothers' business, but felt his fortunes lay elsewhere. He left South Bend in 1853, embarking on a four-month journey to Hangtown, California, and the California Gold Rush. While J.M.'s mining gains were few, he made a small fortune selling wheelbarrows to fellow prospectors. He returned to South Bend in 1858 upon learning his brothers' business was desperate for capital.

The panic of 1857 found H & C Studebaker long on extended credit and short on cash. H & C Studebaker accepted an order in that year from the George Milburn Wagon Company of Mishawaka for army wagons destined for the "Mormon War" in Utah.

Henry and Clement Studebaker expanded their shop to fulfill the contract, but the nation's financial distress left cash money in short supply.

Upon his arrival from California, J.M. Studebaker invested nearly $8,000 in his brothers' business, buying out elder brother Henry Studebaker's share of the firm.

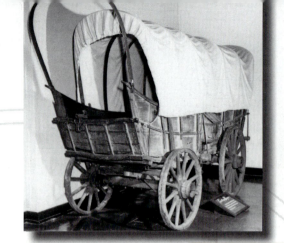
*The Studebaker family's c. 1835 Conestoga wagon.*

*The Studebaker National Museum's blacksmith shop display.*

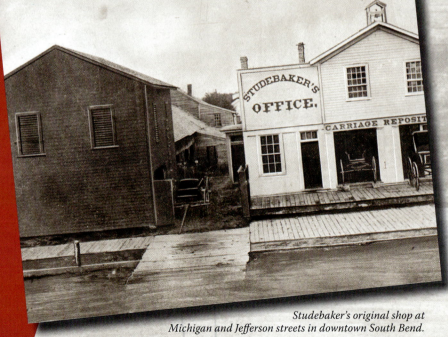
*Studebaker's original shop at Michigan and Jefferson streets in downtown South Bend.*

# Chapter Two: Wait for the Wagon

*Artwork from Studebaker's "Wait For the Wagon" sheet music.*

# The Studebaker Brothers Manufacturing Company

J.M. Studebaker's $8,000 investment allowed H & C Studebaker to further expand its factory. A steady stream of government contracts kept the shop busy during the Civil War as the company churned out wagons for the Union Army.

Peter Studebaker joined the company in 1863. He was a shopkeeper in nearby Goshen, Indiana and was placed in charge of sales in his brothers' company. His agreement with elder brother Clement stated: "I, Peter Studebaker, agree to sell all the wagons my brother Clem can make." Clem's agreement read, "I, Clement Studebaker agree to make all the wagons my brother Peter can sell."

Jacob Studebaker, the youngest of the five brothers, joined the company in 1868. A graduate of the University of Notre Dame, he was placed in charge of the Carriage Department.

The company also took on a new name in 1868: The Studebaker Brothers Manufacturing Company.

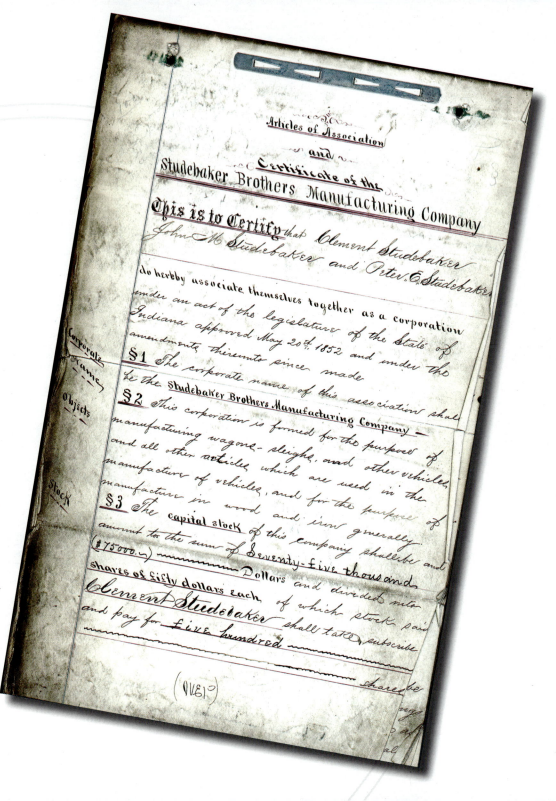

## C. 1863 Hearse

H & C Studebaker offered a wide variety of passenger and commercial vehicles. Studebaker produced a number of hearses in both its horse-drawn and automobile eras.

This hearse was owned by South Bend's Forest G. Hay Funeral Home, and features sterling silver candlesticks and fringed curtains in the casket compartment. The casket compartment has curved glass doors front and rear, and access from below via a trap door.

Studebaker offered horse-drawn "undertaker's wagons" until the turn of the century. During the 1920s and 1930s Studebaker again produced funeral vehicles, this time based on Studebaker's passenger cars.

*Gift of Mrs. Ralph F. Hay.*

*The casket area features a trap door to allow access for cleaning.*

*Undertaker's Wagon c.1900.*

STUDEBAKER NATIONAL MUSEUM | 11

The original Studebaker blacksmith shop site at the corner of Michigan and Jefferson Streets in downtown South Bend had served the company well, but was quickly outgrown as demand increased. Work began in the early 1870s on a new factory located on South Bend's southwest side. By the late 1880s, the Studebaker Brothers Manufacturing Company was the world's largest manufacturer of horse-drawn equipment.

Studebaker's on-site lumber yards supplied raw materials for the newly designated "Plant 1." The Jefferson Street factory continued producing carriages until the early 1890s.

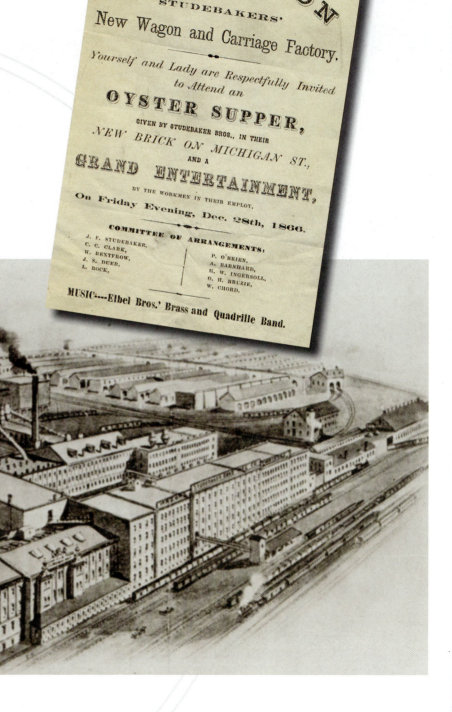

*The Studebaker Bros. Manufacturing Company c. 1880*

# Fire

In both 1872 and 1874, large fires decimated the Studebaker factory.

Following the 1872 conflagration, the city of South Bend installed a new standpipe water system. The decision was made over the objections of Clem and J.M. Studebaker.

The Studebakers, fresh from rebuilding their wagon works, felt that the system was inadequate for the city's needs. To demonstrate his objections, J.M. wagered a cow with the city council's leading standpipe advocate that firemen could not reach the cupola atop the Studebaker administration building with water propelled from their fire hoses.

*The Studebaker Bros.' Wagon Works, with View of the Ruins, the Unburned Buildings, Lumber Sheds, Etc.*

On Christmas Day, 1873, Mr. Studebaker and then United States Vice President Schuyler Colfax ascended the five stories to the cupola and promptly received a thorough drenching courtesy of the local fire fighting brigade. The cow was escorted through downtown South Bend, much to the amusement and delight of onlookers, and then auctioned off for charity.

## STUDEBAKER WORLD WIDE

"The Sun Always Shines on the Studebaker" proclaimed an early Studebaker advertisement. The ad was no empty claim, as the Studebaker name was not an unfamiliar one in foreign lands. The company won awards of merit at Expositions in Madrid, Spain, and Lisbon, Portugal, in 1877. In 1881, an order was received to ship 100 wagons to Africa. The *Salt Lake Herald* reported,

*"…from the general satisfaction that these wagons give in Utah … Africa will no doubt fully appreciate the Studebaker wagon. Since it will stand the dry climate and rough roads of Utah, it should give ample satisfaction in any other country."*

The report went on to state that Studebaker also received an order from the Belgian government for a "fine carriage."

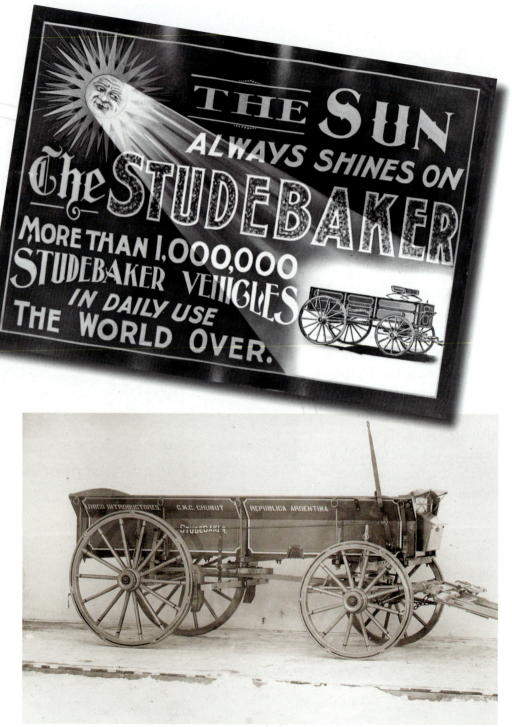

*Carriage catalog from Studebaker's San Francisco Repository c.1890.*

*Studebaker built this Farm Wagon variant specifically for a customer in Argentina c. 1910.*

*A Studebaker wagon sold by the P. Huffsmith dealer of Greeley, Colorado, carries over 16,000 lbs. of potatoes.*

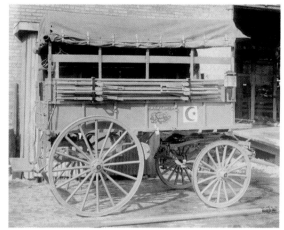
*Military ambulance destined for Turkey c.1910.*

*Ambulance for the French Army, 1915.*

Additional overseas sales complemented a bustling domestic market. The Studebaker Brothers Manufacturing Company's sales department, headed by Peter Studebaker, maintained a powerful dealer network from coast to coast. To supply its dealers, Studebaker established repositories, a combination warehouse/retail outlet/production facility in many major U.S. cities. In 1887, the Studebaker Brothers Manufacturing Company exceeded $2 million in sales for the first time.

*Studebaker's first Administration Building was located on the west side of Lafayette Boulevard just north of Bronson Avenue.*

## The Lincoln Carriage

In 1890, Clement Studebaker purchased the carriage President Abraham Lincoln took to Ford's Theatre the night of his assassination. Mr. Studebaker acquired the carriage with the blessing of Robert Todd Lincoln and placed it on display at the company's Chicago Repository.

A history of the carriage authored by Robert Lincoln states that it was produced by the Wood Brothers in early 1865 and presented to President Lincoln by a group of New York citizens shortly after his second inauguration.

The Lincoln Carriage underwent an extensive conservation treatment in 2007. Conservators stabilized at-risk areas and repaired previous damage. Additionally, the treatment uncovered Lincoln's monogram found on each door, and revealed areas of the carriage's original finishes.

*From the original Studebaker Collection.*

*Abraham Lincoln's dual "AL" monogram. The second AL mirrors the first.*

*Original striping patterns were uncovered on the right rear spring.*

*Wood Brothers' inscription is located on the front wheel hubs.*

The Studebaker Brothers Manufacturing Company's Chicago Repository. The Repository was on Michigan Avenue, and is better known today as the Fine Arts Building. The Lincoln Carriage is highlighted in the circle.

*The Lincoln Carriage was manufactured by the Wood Brothers of New York.*

# The Lafayette Carriage

Marie Joseph Paul Yves Roch Gilbert du Motier, better known as the Marquis de Lafayette was one of many heroes of the United States Revolutionary War. The native Frenchman was instrumental in enlisting his country's aid during the Revolution, and helped lead American forces to victory at Yorktown.

He returned to visit the United States in 1824 at the invitation of President James Monroe. To honor the occasion, a lengthy tour of the country was planned by the Untied States Government.

*From the original Studebaker Collection.*

*J.M. Studebaker admires the Lafayette Carriage c.1915.*

The government commissioned John Curlet of Baltimore, Maryland, to build a carriage for Lafayette's tour. The Lafayette carriage remains one of the earliest examples of American carriage-making.

Clement Studebaker purchased the carriage in 1887 in tribute to his country and craft. It was placed on display at Studebaker's Chicago Repository, and remains the oldest artifact in the collection. The repository still stands and is known today as the Fine Arts Building.

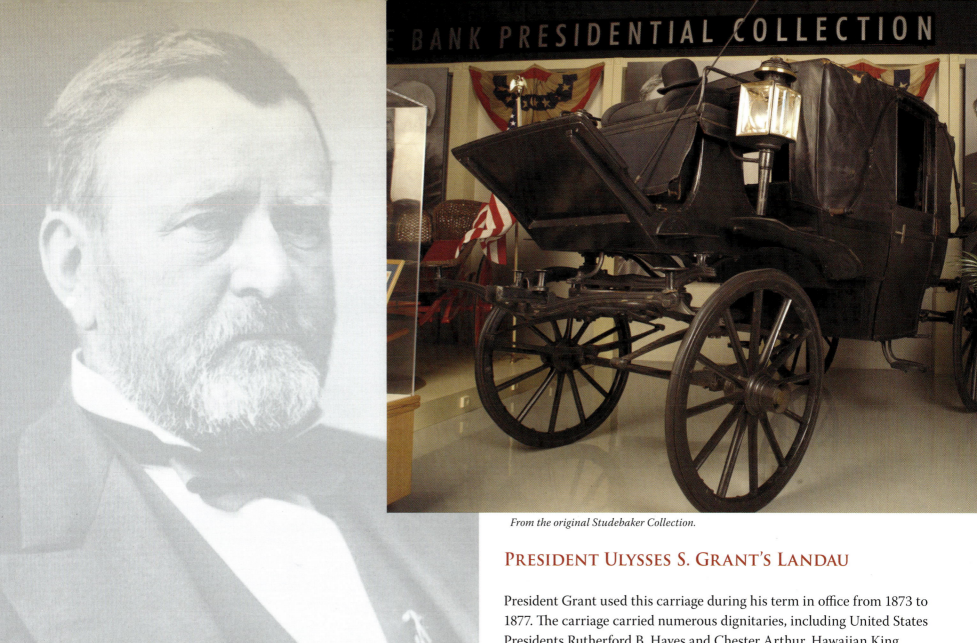

*From the original Studebaker Collection.*

### PRESIDENT ULYSSES S. GRANT'S LANDAU

President Grant used this carriage during his term in office from 1873 to 1877. The carriage carried numerous dignitaries, including United States Presidents Rutherford B. Hayes and Chester Arthur, Hawaiian King Kalakua, and Union Army Generals Philip Sheridan and William Tecumseh Sherman.

This carriage was presented to the original Studebaker collection by Grant's son, General Frederick Dent Grant, on October 2, 1910.

## President Benjamin Harrison's Brougham

The Studebaker Brothers Manufacturing Company built seven carriages for President Harrison. The Studebaker brothers, firm Republicans, strongly supported their fellow Hoosier's presidential campaign.

Once elected, President Harrison placed an order with Studebaker for a supply of carriages and related equipment. Harrison's political adversaries criticized the purchase, and only after public disclosure of the entire order did the hoopla subside.

*From the original Studebaker Collection.*

# The Centennial Wagon

The Centennial Wagon was constructed specifically for the 1876 United States Centennial Exposition in Philadelphia, Pennsylvania. The wagon represented the utmost in skill and craftsmanship ever produced by the 24 year-old firm.

The wheels and running gear are oak, with the seats and wagon box made of the finest birds-eye maple. Period accounts marvelled at the quality of the inlaid rosewood striping and lettering, as many initial examinations of the wagon concluded that the detailing was painted.

*From the original Studebaker Collection.*

Buoyed by the high praise, Studebaker dispatched the Centennial Wagon to Paris for the Paris Exposition of 1878. It took home a silver medal at Paris, and Studebaker was flooded with purchase offers. Studebaker officials steadfastly refused to sell the wagon, declaring it "a memento of the first American Centennial."

*Intertwined initials of the Studebaker Bros. Manufacturing Company are found on the Centennial Wagon's dashboard.*

**STUDEBAKER NATIONAL MUSEUM**

## THE COLUMBIAN EXPOSITION WAGON

For the 1893 Columbian Exposition in Chicago, Studebaker craftsmen built a special farm wagon adorned with medals won at previous contests.

The wagon box itself is rosewood and the running gear is oak. Nearly all the wagon's metal parts are aluminum, a precious metal in the late 19th century. The wagon cost Studebaker over $2,000 to build, a staggering figure when compared to its production counterpart that retailed for about $100.

The "Aluminum Wagon," as it was informally known, took top honors at the Columbian Exposition.

*From the original Studebaker Collection.*

*The Studebaker Brothers Manufacturing Company c.1890.*

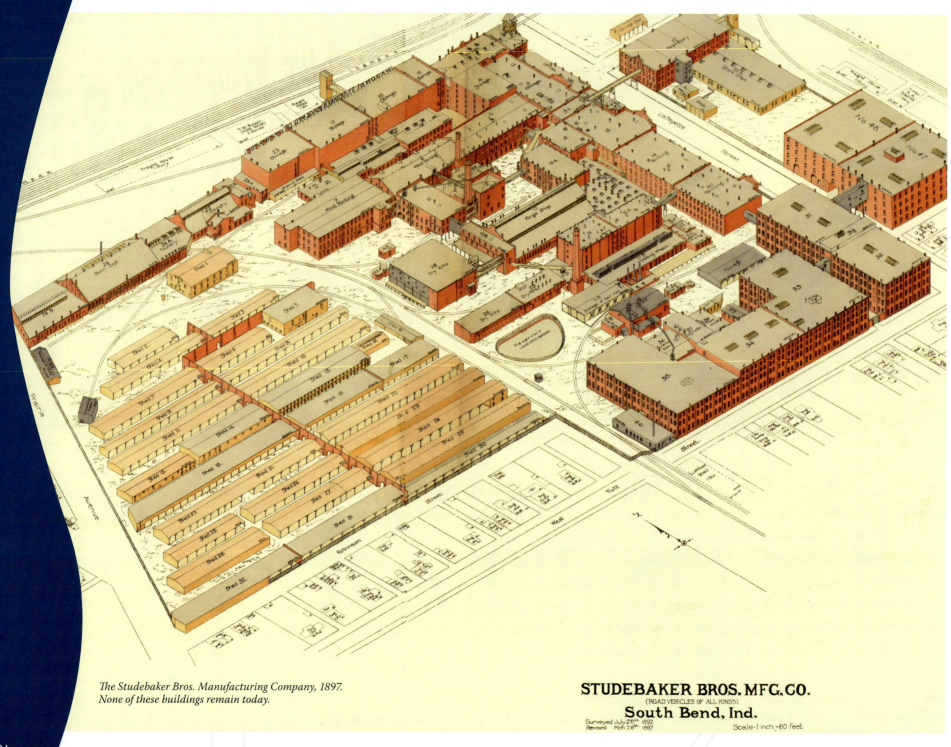

*The Studebaker Bros. Manufacturing Company, 1897. None of these buildings remain today.*

# Chapter 3: Transitions

*Studebaker buildings #58 and #53 c.1915.*

## The Automobile

Frederick Fish was J.M. Studebaker's son-in-law and sat on the Studebaker Brothers Manufacturing Company's Board of Directors. Fish was one of the first "second generation" Studebakers to join the company, and felt that the company should explore automobile production. Despite Fish's enthusiasm, many elder directors remained unconvinced.

A short-lived bicycle craze in the early 1890s left hundreds of upstart bicycle manufacturers bankrupt; some felt the automobile would follow the same path. In addition, sales of horse-drawn equipment remained strong and showed no signs of slowing down. Yet, the growing popularity of the automobile could not be ignored, and the Studebaker Brothers Manufacturing Company's first automobile arrived in 1902.

*Frederick Fish*

J.M. Studebaker declared early gasoline automobiles, "clumsy, dangerous, noisy brutes which stink to high heaven, break down at the worst possible moment, and are a public nuisance." With these sentiments known, it should come as no surprise that the first Studebaker automobile was not powered by gasoline but electricity.

## YOU SHOULD REPLACE THE HORSE WITH STUDEBAKER COMMERCIAL VEHICLES, BECAUSE

1. Cost less to maintain. Horse maintenance charges continue to increase; "Studebaker" upkeep decreasing.
2. Horse a perpetual expense while alive. Must always be fed and groomed, whether at work or idle.
3. Studebaker Electric costs nothing when unemployed.
4. Cuts down stable space required to less than one-half.
5. So compact, can be stabled in smaller quarters, permitting less expensive housing.
6. Requires fewer caretakers.
7. Needs no attention on days when not in use.
8. Lasts longer.
9. Does the work of at least two horse vehicles, and sometimes three.
10. Cuts down expense of drivers and wagon boys.
11. Goes there and back while the horse is on the way.
12. Quicker deliveries; meeting the demands of the times.
13. Working hours of a day not limited.
14. Requires no time for rest.
15. Less hampered and delayed in congested traffic.
16. Garages inoffensive and can be located in convenient places near distributing centers. No insurance restriction.
17. Always ready when you want them.
18. Will work under weather and road conditions when the horse cannot.
19. Can be worked overtime without handicapping efficiency.
20. Requires less space for loading; saves time in loading and unloading. More can be loaded at same time.
21. More cleanly and sanitary.
22. Costs can always be accurately determined and gauged.
23. Makes possible extension of free delivery limits at a lower cost.
24. An indication of progressiveness, and a good advertisement.

*1910 Flanders 20.*

*Starting a gasoline automobile was an occasionally dangerous job requiring a hand crank and quick reflexes.*

In the early years of the automobile industry, more than a few people shared J.M.'s opinion. Electric automobiles were reliable, quiet, and easy to operate.

The typical automobile of the early 1900s was viewed as a novelty rather than a necessity. Open cars dominated the market, and most were priced out of reach of the average citizen. Starting a gasoline automobile was an occasionally dangerous job requiring a hand crank and quick reflexes.

Travel at night or in inclement weather was a hazardous proposition. Roads were rough and poorly marked, maps were inaccurate, and service stations were few and far between.

*Artist's rendering of the new Studebaker Administration Building that opened in 1909. The building still stands at the corner of Main and Bronson Streets in South Bend.*

*Studebaker advertising c.1905.*

*J.M. Studebaker (driving) and an unidentified man pilot a Studebaker electric along a boardwalk "test track" that ran atop the company's factory buildings. H.D. Johnson look on.*

Studebaker's first gasoline-powered automobile debuted in 1904. Instead of plunging head-first into automobiles, Studebaker elected to take a more cautious approach by marketing automobiles made by other companies such as General, Garford, and Everett-Metzger-Flanders (EMF).

These companies offered a ready-made product and production facilities; Studebaker owned a worldwide sales network and a sterling reputation. Satisfied that the automobile was a stable product, Studebaker acquired EMF outright in 1911.

*Studebaker electrics were available in both passenger and commercial models.*

*Thomas Edison and George Mester are pictured in Edison's Studebaker Electric.*

# 1904 Model C

Early Studebaker automobiles were a partnership with the Garford Automobile Company of Elyria, Ohio. Garford produced the chassis and Studebaker supplied the coachwork. Final assembly took place at Studebaker's factory in South Bend.

This vehicle is the oldest gasoline-powered Studebaker in existence, carrying serial number 242.

*Engine:* Opposed two-cylinder, 212 cubic inches.

*Horsepower:* 16

*Price when new:* $1,600

*Gift of the estate of A.E. "Gene" Brim.*

*Coil box and switch.*

## 1909 BACKWARD-FORWARD CAR "PEG"

The U.S. Government purchased two electric-powered eight-passenger vehicles from Studebaker in 1909 to transport Senators from the Senate office building to the United States Capitol Building. The route was through an underground tunnel, which precluded the use of an internal combustion engine.

The two vehicles, nicknamed "Tommy" and "Peg", were called "Backward-Forward" cars as they could be driven in either direction without turning around. Each car was fitted with controls facing in both directions. "Tommy" and "Peg" remained in use until replaced by a rail system in 1915.

*Price when new:* $2,400

*From the original Studebaker Collection.*

*Utah Senator William Henry King sits aboard one of the twin Backward-Forward cars in 1940.*

*"Backward-Forward" cars could be driven in either direction without turning around.*

### 1912 Flanders 20

The Flanders 20 was the price leader in Studebaker's 1912 automobile line. The Flanders featured a rear-mounted transaxle and came with a one-year warranty. Top speed was approximately 40 miles per hour.

This Flanders 20 is from the original Studebaker Collection, and was used in the company's 1964 promotional film, "Different by Design."

*Engine:* Inline four-cylinder

*Horsepower:* 20

*Price when new:* $1,000

*From the original Studebaker Collection.*

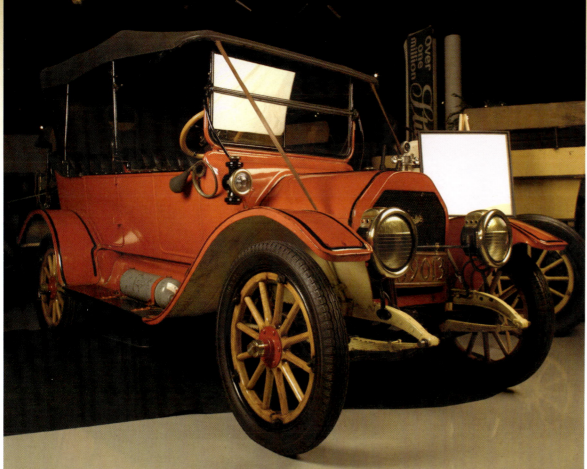

*Gift of Eugene Dana in memory of Charlotte Ann and Ted Dana.*

# 1913 Model 25 Touring Sedan

The 1913 Studebaker line was noted for being exceptionally rugged and reliable. The Model 25 Touring Sedan is powered by a four-cylinder engine, and takes its name from its horsepower rating. Studebaker produced over 35,000 automobiles in 1913.

The tank found on this car's running board supplies acetylene to fuel the headlights.

*Engine:* Inline four-cylinder.

*Horsepower:* 25

*Price when new:* $885

STUDEBAKER NATIONAL MUSEUM

## Studebaker and Detroit

The purchase of EMF bought Studebaker a substantial presence in Detroit, Michigan. EMF owned factories along the Detroit River at Clark and Jefferson Streets as well as another plant on Piquette Avenue. Studebaker also acquired the former Ford plant located adjacent to the EMF's Piquette Avenue property at this time.

All pre-1920 Studebaker automobiles were built in Detroit and the company continued to produce certain models there until 1933. Studebaker's last Detroit-built automobile was the Rockne.

The EMF acquisition in 1911 brought significant changes to the Studebaker Brothers Manufacturing Company's corporate structure. New capital for expansion brought new members to Studebaker's board, and the company was rechristened The Studebaker Corporation.

J.M. Studebaker remained as board chairman until his retirement in 1915, and was designated honorary chairman until his death in 1917.

*Studebaker's Jefferson Avenue plant in Detroit. It was razed in the mid 1930s.*

*Studebaker's Piquette Avenue plant in Detroit. The three-story building at the extreme right was purchased from Ford, and was where Henry Ford built the first Model "T."*

# Chapter 4: Evolution

*New factory buildings under construction at Studebaker's South Bend plant in October of 1919.*

## ALBERT RUSSELL ERSKINE

The reigns passed to Huntsville, Alabama, native Albert Russell Erskine. Erskine was a newcomer to Studebaker, with previous stops at the American Cotton Company, Yale and Towne Manufacturing, and Underwood Typewriter. Erskine joined the company as Treasurer in 1911, and assumed the presidency in 1915. His selection as President marked the first time a non-family member would lead the Studebaker Corporation.

Erskine was quoted as saying, "I eat obstacles for breakfast." His strong personality and aggressive management style left an indelible mark on Studebaker history. The company experienced over a decade of growth and expansion during Erskine's tenure, accompanied by record sales and profits. Yet, Erskine's misjudgment of the Great Depression nearly cost Studebaker its life.

*Albert Russell Erskine*

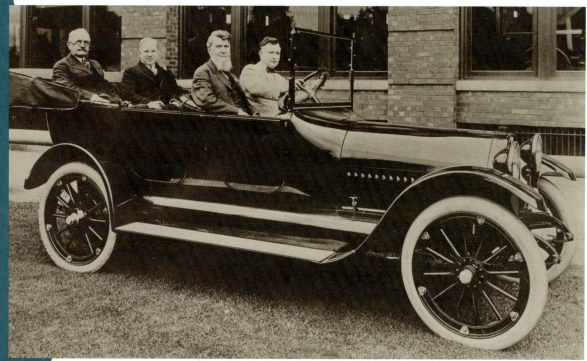
L-R: Frederick Fish, Albert Erskine, John M. Studebaker, and Studebaker vice-president James Heaslet.

# 1916 Four-Forty Roadster

Studebaker's 1916 offerings featured both four and six-cylinder models. The Roadster was Studebaker's most popular model, and featured a vacuum-tank fuel system, leather interior, and a three-speed transmission. This Roadster was restored by the Studebaker National Museum's volunteer corps and completed in 2003.

*Engine:* Inline four-cylinder, 233 cubic inches.
*Horsepower:* 40
*Price when new:* $885

*Gift of Mr. Greg Barger.*

*Advertising card, 1916.*

STUDEBAKER NATIONAL MUSEUM

## 1919 Big Six

On June 13, 1918, Mr. Fenton Norman of Santa Barbara, California, took delivery of a new Studebaker Big Six Touring car at the Joe Stewart dealership in Ventura, California. Over the next two years, Mr. Norman travelled 94,000 miles in his Big Six.

The Associated Transit Company of Los Angeles, California, purchased the car in 1920. Associated Transit distributed newspapers throughout the Los Angeles area. Six days a week the Big Six carried 1500 lbs. of paper and pulled a 2,000-pound trailer on its 400-mile route.

By 1923, the Big Six had logged over 390,000 miles. Studebaker purchased the car in 1924, and dispatched it on a cross-country promotional tour touting Studebaker's outstanding durability.

*Engine:* Inline six-cylinder, 353 cubic inches.
*Horsepower:* 60
*Price when new:* $2,000

*"…the car averaged 14 miles per gallon of gasoline, and approximately 1000 miles per gallon of oil."*
—Mr. Fenton Norman

*From the original Studebaker Collection.*

*The 1919 Big Six on its cross-country tour, 1924.*

## 1919 Izzer Buggy

The Izzer buggy got its name from a conversation overheard by Peter Studebaker at a horse auction. A gentleman was extolling an animal's previous accomplishments when the potential buyer interjected, "I don't want a wuzzer, I want an Izzer!" It was the horse's current health that mattered to the buyer, not its past glories.

Peter Studebaker was impressed with the buyer's savvy, and named Studebaker's new buggy the "Izzer." This Izzer buggy is the last buggy manufactured by the Studebaker Corporation.

*"Studebaker" script is located on the rear of the Izzer's body.*

*From the original Studebaker Collection.*

*"I don't want a wuzzer, I want an Izzer!"*

STUDEBAKER NATIONAL MUSEUM | 39

## 1920 Farm Wagon

In 1920, Studebaker sold its remaining horse-drawn business to the Kentucky Wagon Manufacturing Company of Louisville, Kentucky.

Studebaker Farm Wagons were available in a wide variety of models and optional equipment. The last Farm Wagon joined the company collection following its completion in late 1920.

*Price when new:* $130

*From the original Studebaker Collection.*

*Studebaker letterhead c.1900.*

*Advertisments for the Studebaker Farm Wagon c.1910.*

## A New Factory

One of Albert Erskine's major decisions was to discontinue horse-drawn vehicles and centralize automobile production in South Bend.

A massive building campaign was already underway when Studebaker liquidated its remaining horse-drawn business in 1920. New steel-and-concrete buildings replaced the Studebaker lumber sheds as the entire plant retooled for automobile production.

*The central section of buildings 47, 47A, 48, and 48A dated to the 1890s. These structures were later known locally as the Transwestern Building. They were razed in the mid 1980s.*

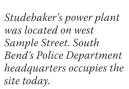

*Studebaker's power plant was located on west Sample Street. South Bend's Police Department headquarters occupies the site today.*

By the end of the decade, Studebaker's South Bend factory featured new buildings for body production and final assembly, a state-of-the-art foundry and machine shop, as well as a new engineering building and an 800-acre outdoor testing facility.

*Studebaker's new body assembly building, 1923. This building stands on the site of Studebaker's first Administration Building (see page 15).*

*A crew of workers lay end-block flooring in one of Studebaker's new factory buildings c.1923.*

## 1920 Light Six

The Light Six debuted in 1920, and was the first Studebaker automobile produced entirely in South Bend.

This Light Six bears serial number 1,000,001 and shows but 19 miles on the odometer. Like the last Farm Wagon, the first Light Six was immediately placed in Studebaker's company museum.

*Engine:* Inline six-cylinder, 207 cubic inches.
*Horsepower:* 40
*Price when new:* $1,485

*From the original Studebaker Collection.*

*The 1920 Light Six was the first Studebaker automobile built entirely in South Bend.*

*Gift of the estate of George Goodrich.*

## 1924 Light Six

This Light Six features custom coachwork by the Shanghai Horse Bazaar and Automobile Company of Shanghai, China. The Shanghai Horse Bazaar and Automobile Company was a Studebaker agency and manufactured custom bodies for automobiles of all makes.

Coy Goodrich, a Studebaker agent in China, managed the automobile operations of the Shanghai Horse Bazaar Co. from 1916-1923 and commissioned this body in early 1923. Following his tenure in China, Goodrich had the body shipped to San Francisco where it was mated to a 1924 Studebaker Light Six chassis.

The body is made entirely of aluminum, with a fold-out windshield and built-in visor. The interior is trimmed in teak with mohair upholstery.

*Engine:* Inline six-cylinder, 207 cubic inches.
*Horsepower:* 40

### 1926 BIG SIX DUPLEX PHAETON

In the early 1920s, sales of open cars greatly outpaced those of closed models. Open cars were less expensive, and, prior to the advent of safety glass, perceived as safer than their sedan counterparts. Studebaker introduced the Duplex Phaeton in 1925 in an attempt to capture the advantages of both.

The Duplex featured the open qualities of a touring car and the all-weather capabilities of a sedan. The top was fixed, with pull-down side curtains similar to window shades. The Duplex Phaeton and its sibling Duplex Roadster body styles were unique to Studebaker, and only produced in 1925 and 1926.

*Engine:* Inline six-cylinder, 353 cubic inches.

*Horsepower:* 75

*Price when new:* $1,875

*The Duplex Phaeton was a Studebaker exclusive.*

*Gift of Mr. Woodson Allen.*

## 1927 President Limousine

Studebaker's prestigious President model debuted in 1927. The President was initially only available as a seven-passenger sedan, but the line was soon expanded to include a variety of body styles.

Nineteen twenty-seven was the only year Studebaker's President was powered by a six-cylinder engine, as all subsequent offerings featured eight-cylinder powerplants.

This Limousine is the only restored example known to exist, and features a divider window and rear passenger jump seats.

*Engine:* Inline six-cylinder, 353 cubic inches.
*Horsepower:* 75
*Price when new:* $2,345

*Gift of Mr. Victor Tomasso.*

*Studebaker's radiator mascot "Atalanta."*

*This Limousine is the only restored example known to exist.*

**STUDEBAKER NATIONAL MUSEUM** | 47

## The Proving Ground

The Studebaker Proving Ground opened in late 1926 eight miles west of South Bend on State Highway 2. It was here that Studebaker cars and trucks were subjected to every possible test of endurance and quality. The facility included a three mile high-speed oval, terrain of every conceivable type, a comprehensive garage and repair center, and a two-story clubhouse for use by Studebaker employees. To identify the property to air travelers, pine trees spelling out **"STUDEBAKER"** were planted in 1937 and remain visible to the present day.

Studebaker sold the Proving Ground to Bendix in the 1960s, who in turn gave a portion of the land to St. Joseph County for use as a park. The remaining portion is still in use as a testing facility by the Robert Bosch Corporation.

*Water testing the 1950 models.*

*A 1947 Champion ascends a 30% grade.*

*Studebaker engineers measure the turning circle on a 1929 Dictator. The Proving Ground Clubhouse can be seen in the background.*

## THE BIG PRESIDENT

The Proving Ground was home to the boldest advertisement ever created by the Studebaker Corporation. In the early spring of 1930, Paul Auman, head of Studebaker's experimental body shop, received an assignment to create a model of the soon to be introduced 1931 President Four Season Roadster.

The catch was that the model was to be two and one half times normal size. Upon completion, the giant President was just over 40 feet long and 14 feet high. It was situated atop a grassy knoll 100 yards west of the main gate.

Each body panel was painstakingly made of white pine in the Studebaker factory shops in South Bend and transported out to the Proving Ground for assembly. The wire wheel spokes were made from electrical conduit, and Firestone provided special ten-foot tires.

The car was reproduced in exacting detail, featuring the same number of hood louvers and wheel spokes as its normal size counterpart. The only major discrepancy was the big car used a rear-mounted spare tire, while all production 1931 President Four Season Roadsters used side mounted spares.

STUDEBAKER NATIONAL MUSEUM | 49

To put all of this into perspective, a cutout of a man with a sign reading "This Man is Six Feet Tall" stood near the front bumper.

By 1936, the big President no longer resembled current models, and South Bend's harsh winters had taken their toll on the largely wooden automobile.

In spring of 1936, the hubcaps and two tires were removed, and the car was doused in an accelerant and ignited. In less than half an hour, the President was reduced to ashes.

*In less than half an hour, the President was reduced to ashes.*

## The Rockne

Under Erskine's able leadership, sales mounted with each succeeding year. Studebaker sought to expand its markets in the late 1920s, introducing the entry-level Erskine automobile in 1927 and purchasing luxury manufacturer Pierce-Arrow in 1928.

Notre Dame Football coach Knute Rockne joined the Studebaker Sales Department that same year as a company spokesman and motivational speaker.

# ROCKNE

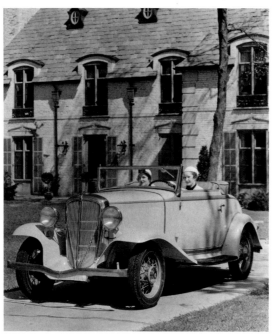
*1932 Rockne Convertible Coupe.*

*Knute Rockne greets representatives from San Francisco's Chester Weaver Studebaker dealership in front of a 1931 Studebaker Six.*

*Coach Rockne and his 1927 Dictator.*

Rockne was rumored to be considering leaving coaching to work at Studebaker full time. His true plans were never made public as he tragically perished in a plane crash on March 31, 1931.

The Erskine automobile failed in its quest to establish a foothold in the low-priced field and was phased out in 1930. Studebaker tried once again in mid 1932 with the Rockne.

The Rockne was by all accounts a fine automobile, but stood little chance to succeed in the throes of the Great Depression. The Rockne was discontinued after 1933.

# 1927 Commander Sedan

Studebaker began extensive speed and endurance testing in 1927. In September of that year, this Commander established a new transcontinental record by traveling from New York to San Francisco in 77 hours and 40 minutes. The driver, Ab Jenkins, was a building contractor by trade and pursued endurance driving as a hobby.

*From the original Studebaker Collection.*

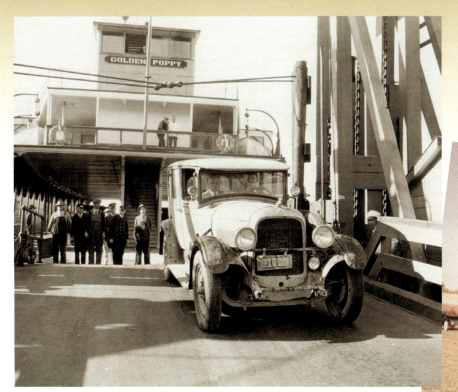

*Ab Jenkins disembarks from the Golden Gate Ferry in San Francisco 77 hours and 40 minutes after leaving New York City.*

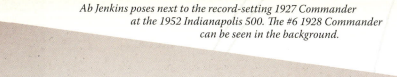

*Ab Jenkins poses next to the record-setting 1927 Commander at the 1952 Indianapolis 500. The #6 1928 Commander can be seen in the background.*

*David Abbot "Ab" Jenkins, Albert Erskine, and Sheriff Grover Sexton of Yavapai County, Arizona pose in front of Jenkins' 1926 Studebaker Big Six. This car held the transcontinental record until it was broken by Jenkins in the 1927 Commander Sedan.*

The record he broke was his own, set one year earlier in a 1926 Studebaker. Jenkins' trip was over public roads, and speed limits, when present, were strictly observed.

*Engine:* Inline six-cylinder, 353 cubic inches.

*Horsepower:* 75

*Price when new:* $1,595

## 1928 Commander Roadster

On a rainy October day in 1927 on a dilapidated board race track near Atlantic City, New Jersey, three Studebaker Commanders set out to complete 25,000 miles as quickly as possible. The trio of Commanders lapped the track for sixteen days. The clock ran continuously during the event, even during driver changes and pit stops.

*The #6 Commander falls victim to a hole in the track.*

*Studebaker's record-setting runs were hampered by the poor condition of the board race track.*

*From the original Studebaker Collection.*

The #6 Commander Roadster completed the 25,000 miles first at an average of over 65 miles per hour. Following the campaign the #6 car crisscrossed the country visiting Studebaker dealers.

*Engine:* Inline six-cylinder, 353 cubic inches.

*Horsepower:* 85

*Price when new:* $1,510

*The #6 Commander made numerous promotional stops at Studebaker dealers throughout the country.*

STUDEBAKER NATIONAL MUSEUM | 55

## 1928 Studebaker Fire Truck

This fire truck was purchased new by the St. Joseph, Michigan Fire Department. Studebaker supplied the chassis, which was then outfitted by the Boyer Fire Apparatus Company of Logansport, Indiana.

Studebaker supplied chassis for fire truck use until truck production ceased in December of 1963. This truck was restored by the Studebaker National Museum volunteers corps.

*Engine:* Inline six-cylinder, 353 cubic inches.

*Horsepower:* 75

*Price when new:* $2,410

*Gift of Burkhart Advertising.*

*South Bend's Fire Chief poses next to his new 1916 Studebaker outside South Bend Fire Station #1.*

*Hub cap and wheel striping, 1928 Fire Truck.*

## 1931 Studebaker Six Roadster

The Studebaker Six was the company's entry level model in 1931. All 1931 Studebaker automobiles featured Free Wheeling, which allowed the car to coast when vehicle speed was greater than engine speed.

1931 was also the first year that a radio was offered as a factory-approved accessory. This 1931 Studebaker Six is formerly of the S. Ray Miller Museum of Elkhart, Indiana.

*Engine:* Inline six-cylinder, 205 cubic inches.
*Horsepower:* 70
*Price when new:* $795

Gift of Mr. Mike Arnold, Mr. Najeeb Khan, Mr. Richard Lavanture, Mr. Mike Leep, Mr. Pat Ruszkowski, and Dr. Mark Smucker.

This Studebaker Six is fitted with Pilot-Ray driving lights that turn left or right with the front wheels.

"Les Preludes" was one of Studebaker's 1931 radiator mascots.

# The "500"

Studebaker's racing and endurance campaigns neatly coincided with rule changes for the 1930 Indianapolis 500. The previous years' 500s had been the domain of specialty-built race cars, but the new regulations opened the door to production-based entries with "stock" components.

The success of privately-entered Studebaker-powered cars in the 1930 and 1931 500s led to a factory-backed five-car effort for 1932 and 1933.

*Studebaker's 1932 Indianapolis 500 team.*

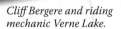

*Cliff Bergere and riding mechanic Verne Lake.*

*Studebaker's 1933 team featured new streamlined bodies on four of the five cars.*

The Studebaker racers were built largely with off-the-shelf components and were advertised as being "85% stock". Engines were sourced from the Studebaker President, brakes came from the Studebaker Six.

*Studebaker's 1933 team at speed.*

*George Hunt (left background), Tony Gulotta (far right) and two unidentified gentlemen are hard at work on three of Studebaker's 1932 race cars.*

*Practice session at the 1933 Indianapolis 500.*

*Riding mechanic Walter Mitchell vaults out of the #37 car during a practice pit stop at the 1932 500.*

The Studebaker team's best finish was third in 1932, and all five cars finished in the top 12 in 1933.

*Studebaker received $13,000 in prize money in 1932. Private sponsors often paid small sums to lap leaders.*

*Racing is dirty work, as driver Tony Gulotta and riding mechanic Carl Riscignio can attest.*

*Cliff Bergere inspects his goggles as riding mechanic Verne Lake approaches just prior to the start of the 1933 Indianapolis 500.*

*The 1933 drivers (L-R): Zeke Meyer, L.L Corum, Tony Gulotta, Luther Johnson, and Cliff Bergere.*

# 1932 President Convertible Coupe

Studebaker's entire line received a makeover in 1932. New streamlined bodies were introduced, along with many mechanical improvements such as upgraded shock absorbers and synchronized transmissions. Also new for 1932 was the Startix self-starting system which automatically restarted the engine in case of a stall.

All 1929-1932 Studebaker Presidents and 1933 Speedway Presidents are certified as Full Classics® by the Classic Car Club of America. Fewer than ten 1932 President Convertible Coupes remain today.

*Engine:* Inline eight-cylinder, 337 cubic inches.

*Horsepower:* 122

*Price when new:* $1,940

*Gift in memory of Carroll and Verneda Studebaker by Cathy Davis Studebaker and family.*

*1932 sales literature.*

*Fewer than ten 1932 President Convertible Coupes remain today.*

## Receivership

Despite its racing success, Studebaker could not escape the harsh realities of the Great Depression. Studebaker's sales fell precipitously from 1929 through 1933.

Like many business leaders, Albert Erskine underestimated the severity of the Depression. In an effort to maintain Studebaker stock prices, Erskine authorized dividend payments even when Studebaker did not show a profit. This policy had a devastating effect on Studebaker's cash reserves, as 1933 dividends exceeded profits by 500%.

The final blow came on March 21, 1933. With liquid funds depleted, the Studebaker Corporation was forced into receivership, a form of corporate bankruptcy.

The eighty-one year-old company's survival lay in the hands of U.S. District Court Judge Thomas Slick. Slick and Erskine had a history dating to 1925, when Erskine vocally opposed Slick's candidacy for the bench.

In reviewing the case, Slick appointed Studebaker vice presidents Paul Hoffman and Harold Vance and White Motors Chairman Ashton Bean as receivers. Bean's appointment was due to Studebaker's holding of a significant amount of White stock. Day to day operations fell to Hoffman and Vance. Erskine was not allowed any part in Studebaker's reorganization.

Compounding this difficult time in Erskine's life was an outstanding personal income tax liability in excess of $700,000 as well as deteriorating health.

On July 1st, 1933, Albert Erskine died in his South Bend home of a self-inflicted gunshot wound. He left a note for his son that stated, "I cannot go on any longer."

# Chapter 5: Recovery

*A parade of 1935 Studebakers celebrate the company's emergence from receivership. This view looks south on Michigan Street at Washington Street in downtown South Bend.*

## HOFFMAN AND VANCE

Paul Hoffman and Harold Vance came from very different backgrounds. Vance began his tenure with Studebaker in 1910 as a mechanic's apprentice, while Hoffman hailed from California and owned several Studebaker dealerships. Both men quickly rose through the ranks, with Hoffman being named Vice President of Sales in 1925 and Vance appointed Vice President of Production and Engineering in 1926.

Hoffman and Vance faced a daunting task and wasted no time in righting the ship. Pierce-Arrow was sold, all remaining Detroit operations were transferred to South Bend, the racing program was canceled, and Studebaker's model lineup was significantly scaled back.

After a layoff of over a month, production resumed in April of 1933. Studebaker launched an advertising campaign proclaiming, "Studebaker Carries On" to further quell rumors of its demise.

Hoffman and Vance's efforts came to fruition on March 1, 1935, when Studebaker officially emerged from receivership.

*Paul Hoffman and Harold Vance.*

## 1934 Bendix SWC

The Bendix name is well-known in the automotive industry. Vincent Bendix's development of the self-named "Bendix" starter drive in the early 'teens made his company into one of the industry's major component suppliers.

The South Bend based Bendix grew to include over 100 subsidiaries that supplied brakes, carburetors, and many other products to the industry.

*Engine:* Inline six-cylinder, 170 cubic inches.
*Engine manufacturer:* Continental
*Horsepower:* 86
*Cost to build:* $84,000

*Gift of the Honeywell Corporation.*

**STUDEBAKER NATIONAL MUSEUM**

The Steel Wheel Corporation (SWC) existed only on paper, and its sole purpose was to "build" a Bendix automobile. The car was built entirely by hand, and featured nearly every automotive product Bendix produced. The car was shown in Europe but never in the United States, as Vincent Bendix did not want his largest customers to think he was entering into competition with them. The car carries no Bendix badging; the only identifying logos are of the Steel Wheel Corporation.

General Motors acquired Bendix shortly after the car's completion and halted all work on the project. After years in storage, the car was rediscovered in the late 1960s. In 1977, it was placed on display with the Studebaker collection at South Bend's new Century Center convention facility.

The car remained on display with the Studebaker collection, but was owned by Bendix until the 1980s. After a series of mergers and acquisitions, the car became property of the Honeywell Corporation. Honeywell gifted the Bendix car to the Studebaker National Museum in October of 2005.

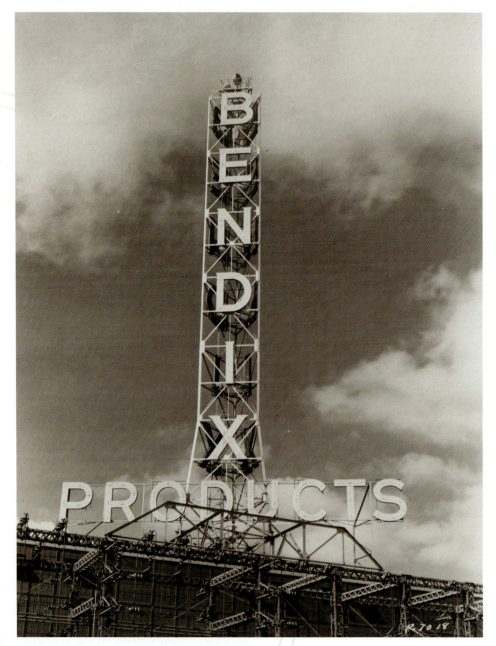

*The Bendix plant c.1950.*

# 1935 Commander Roadster

Studebaker's 1935 automobiles featured many major mechanical and safety improvements. Four-wheel hydraulic brakes and safety glass were now standard, with independent front suspension available at extra cost.

This Commander appeared in the movie "The Color Purple." Yellow paint was not a regular production option, but was available on special order for an additional $15.

*Engine:* Inline eight-cylinder, 250 cubic inches.
*Horsepower:* 107
*Price when new:* $895

*Exhibited through the courtesy of Dr. George Vassos.*

*Advertising photo, 1935.*

## STARS AND THEIR CARS

Like any diligent company, Studebaker frequently employed celebrities to promote its products. Additionally, numerous celebrities and notables favored Studebakers for their daily transportation, including Eleanor Roosevelt, Ed Sullivan, Art Linkletter, and Judy Garland.

*Boxer Joe Louis poses with a 1937 President.*

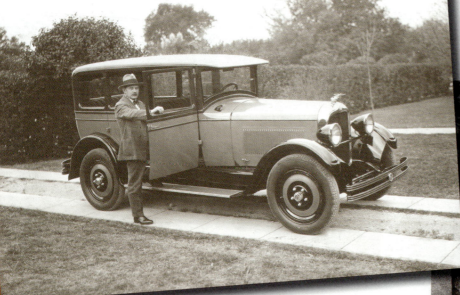
*Mt. Rushmore creator Gutzon Borglum and his 1927 Commander.*

*Mickey Rooney and a 1935 Commander Land Cruiser.*

*James Bond novelist Ian Fleming and his Avanti.*

*David Abbot "Ab" Jenkins and Babe Ruth pose with a 1931 President Four Season Roadster.*

*Television personality Art Linkletter in his 1948 Champion convertible.*

Former Presidents Jimmy Carter and George H.W. Bush were also proud Studebaker owners, as was Gutzon Borglum, creator of Mt. Rushmore, and "James Bond" novelist Ian Fleming.

*Golfer Byron Nelson and his 1941 President Skyway Land Cruiser.*

## 1937 Coupe Express

Studebaker's new-for-1937 Coupe Express drew its styling from Studebaker's passenger car models, much like the later Chevrolet El Camino.

The chassis and interior appointments were taken from the 1937 Dictator, as were many of the body components. Despite its popularity today, the car-based Coupe Express was never a sales success, and was only built from 1937-1939.

*Engine:* Inline six-cylinder, 218 cubic inches.
*Horsepower:* 90
*Price when new:* $670

*Gift of Mr. Jack Merrill.*

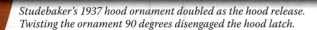

*Studebaker's 1937 hood ornament doubled as the hood release. Twisting the ornament 90 degrees disengaged the hood latch.*

# Raymond Loewy

In 1936, Studebaker retained Raymond Loewy Associates to head the Studebaker Design Department. Under Loewy's leadership, Studebaker earned a lasting reputation as a leader in automotive design.

The French-born Loewy came to the United States in 1919. He was a talented fashion designer and illustrator, which led to work with Harper's and Vogue magazines.

*Raymond Loewy c.1940.*

Loewy moved into the fledgling field of industrial design in the late 1920s when he received a contract to redesign the Gestetner Company's duplicating machine. His first automobile assignment came a few years later for the 1934 Hupmobile.

STUDEBAKER NATIONAL MUSEUM

It should be stated that Raymond Loewy did not personally create every design; his role can best be compared to the conductor of a symphony. Loewy was an excellent salesman and also an astute judge of talent.

Studebaker's Design Department alumni included some of the foremost talents in the industry: Gordon Buehrig, creator of the acclaimed Cord 810/812, Virgil Exner, who later went on to head Chrysler's design department, and Robert Bourke, architect of Studebaker's iconic "bullet nose" models as well as the 1953 Starliner hardtop.

*Clockwise, from left front: Nancy Spence (back to camera), Virginia Spence, Frank Alhroth, Vince Gardner, Jake Aldrich, John Reinhart, Audrey Moore, Gordon Buehrig, Holden "Bob" Koto, Robert Bourke, Virgil Exner.*

NEW 1938 STUDEBAKER COMMANDER CLUB SEDAN
For Six Passengers and 20.9 Cubic Feet of Luggage

*Harold Vance and Paul Hoffman admire the new 1939 Champion.*

*1939 President Convertible Sedan.*

## The Champion

The first Loewy-designed Studebakers appeared for the 1938 model year, but it was the 1939 Champion that propelled Loewy's name into the spotlight.

Despite repeated attempts, Studebaker enjoyed precious little success in the low-priced field. The Erskine of 1927 was uncompetitive in both price and quality. The 1932 Rockne was a fine automobile on its own merits, but fell victim to timing and circumstance. Studebaker was determined not to repeat its past failures, and spent three years on research, design, and testing.

The Studebaker Champion was introduced with much fanfare in April of 1939. Prospective buyers encountered a completely new automobile offering exceptional fuel economy without sacrificing comfort or quality.

The petite Champion shared no parts with Studebaker's senior models, and enjoyed a nearly 600-pound weight advantage over its nearest competitors.

L-R: Raymond Loewy, George Matthews, and Robert Bourke.

*The Champion's exhaustive testing regimen included a "steeplechase" course.*

Over 30,000 Champions were sold in 1939's abbreviated run, growing to in excess of 84,000 in 1941. The Champion nearly doubled Studebaker's sales, and gave the company a long-sought foothold in the low-priced market.

*The 1939 Champion was completely new from the ground up.*

Final Assembly, 1940.

## OFF TO WAR

The events of December 1941 brought an end to civilian automobile production as the industry prepared for war. Government restrictions on certain materials brought changes to the 1942 Studebakers even before production ended. Ivory-colored paint was substituted for chromium on trim items, whitewall tires became unavailable, and pistons were now made from cast iron instead of aluminum. Cars so equipped were nicknamed "blackout" models due to their lack of brightwork.

Studebaker designated these "blackout" automobiles as "Series 90" models in honor of the company's 90th birthday. Although the anniversary was noted with traditional celebrations, the company's main focus was converting its factories for defense production. The last prewar civilian Studebaker rolled off the assembly line on January 31, 1942.

*1942 Commander Deluxestyle Cruising Sedan.*

# Chapter 6: Duty

*Studebaker's 1942 literature reflected the nation's preparation for war.*

Studebaker was no stranger to war production. Its first military order was received some 85 years earlier via the Milburn Company of Mishawaka, Indiana. In 1857, the U.S. Government contracted Milburn for several hundred wagons to be used in the so-called "Mormon War" in Utah. Milburn subcontracted 100 of the wagons to H & C Studebaker, who delivered the order in half the time specified.

The onset of the Civil War brought additional business to H & C Studebaker, with the War Department placing its first order in 1862. The Spanish-American war in 1896 saw the U. S. Government order 500 wagons to be delivered in 36 hours. In customary Studebaker fashion, the order was completed and shipped in 24 hours.

Studebaker wagons were also a favorite of the British Army, who in 1899 placed a large order for use in the Boer War in South Africa.

In commenting on the performance of the Studebaker wagons, English General Lord Roberts was quoted as saying, "They proved superior to any other make of either Cape or English manufacturer."

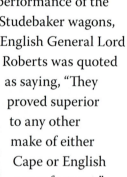

*Supply Wagon, Spanish-American War.*

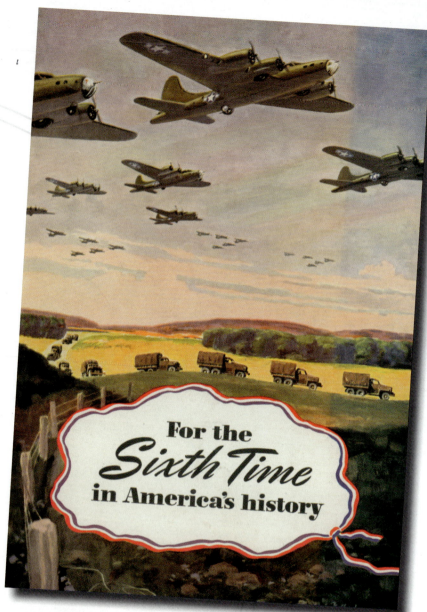

*Studebaker advertising, World War II.*

# The War To End All Wars

When hostilities broke out in Europe in 1914, the British Army purchased 3,000 wagons from the Studebaker Corporation. Additional orders were received from France and Russia. When the United States entered the conflict, Studebaker President Albert Erskine dispatched a telegram to President Woodrow Wilson stating:

*Studebaker factories of course are at the disposal of the Government. Any orders given will receive preference and clear right of way.*

President Wilson responded:

*Thank you for the generous assurances of your telegram of today. I greatly appreciate your pledge of cooperation.*

Thank you for the generous assurances of your telegram of today. I greatly appreciate your pledge of cooperation.

*From the original Studebaker Collection.*

*World War I U.S. Army Ambulance.*

## 1917 Water Cart

Studebaker produced over 10,000 water carts for the U.S. Army during World War I. The carts were used to supply troops with fresh water while in the field. The "USQMC" stenciled on the barrel stands for "United States Quarter Master Corps."

*The "USQMC" stenciled on the barrel stands for "United States Quarter Master Corps."*

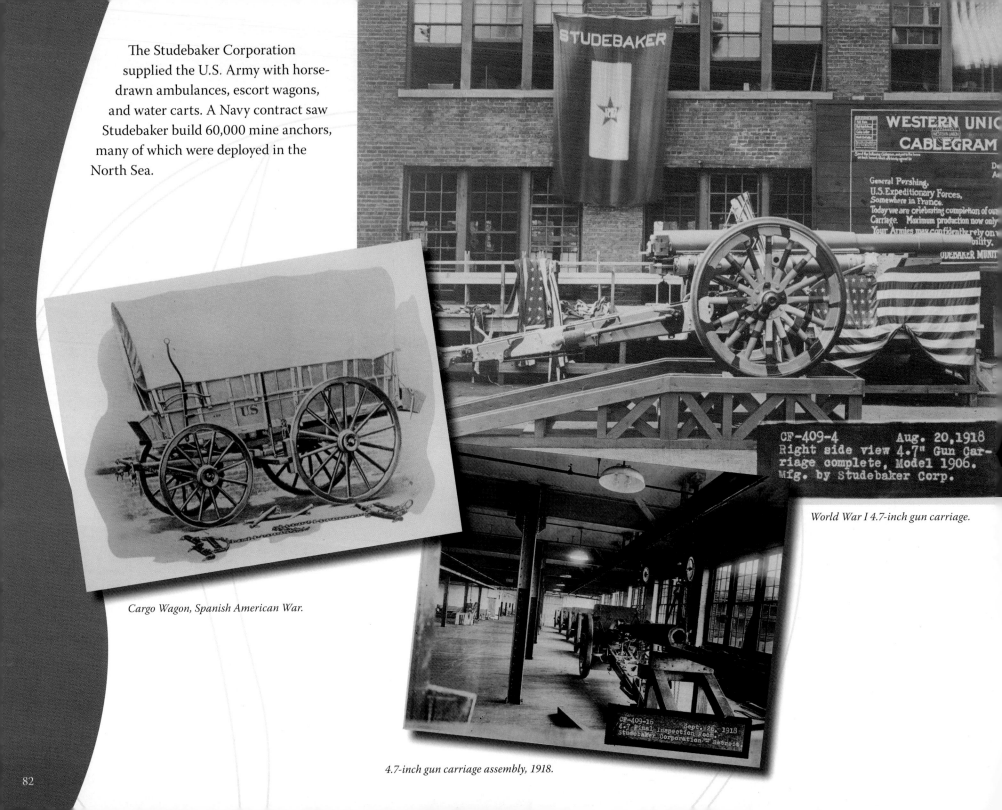

The Studebaker Corporation supplied the U.S. Army with horse-drawn ambulances, escort wagons, and water carts. A Navy contract saw Studebaker build 60,000 mine anchors, many of which were deployed in the North Sea.

*Cargo Wagon, Spanish American War.*

*World War I 4.7-inch gun carriage.*

*4.7-inch gun carriage assembly, 1918.*

## World War II

Horse-drawn equipment gave way to mechanized units for World War II. Studebaker's primary products for World War II included US6 2½-ton trucks, Wright-Cyclone R-1820 airplane engines, and the Weasel.

Studebaker was one of three suppliers of US6 6x4 and 6x6 trucks. By war's end, Studebaker built nearly 200,000 trucks, with many being shipped to Russia for use by the Red Army. The Studebaker-built trucks proved so popular with the Russian troops that the word "Studebaker" became slang for trucks of all kinds.

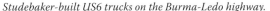
*Studebaker-built US6 trucks on the Burma-Ledo highway.*

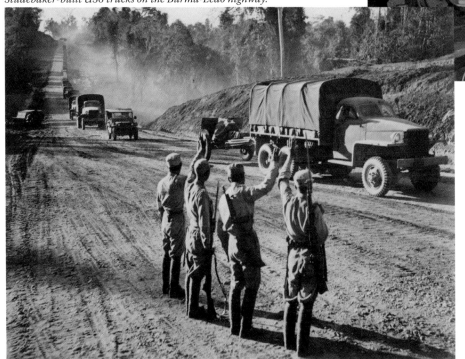
*US6 assembly line.*

*"Studebaker" became a Russian slang term for trucks of all kinds.*

The Wright-Cyclone R-1820 radial engine powered the B17 Flying Fortress and was built at the company's new Chippewa Avenue plant on South Bend's south side.

By the end of the war, Studebaker was the sole supplier of B17 engines, and most airworthy Flying Fortresses today carry at least one Studebaker-built powerplant.

*Engine assembly at the Chippewa Avenue plant.*

**Studebaker is proud of its assignments in the arming of our Nation and its Allies** — Studebaker builds huge quantities of Wright Cyclone engines for the Boeing Flying Fortress as well as much other war matériel including millions of dollars worth of big, multiple-drive military trucks for the forces of the United Nations every week.

*R-1820 radial engine.*

## THE WEASEL

The M28/M29 "Weasel" was Studebaker's response to the U.S. Army's request for an all terrain cargo carrier. It was initially developed for use in snow-covered areas, but proved adept in nearly all topographies.

The Weasel was available in both regular and amphibious configurations.

*Engine:* Inline six-cylinder, 170 cubic inches.

*Horsepower:* 70

*Studebaker engineers snow-tested the Weasel in Michigan's Upper Peninsula.*

*From the original Studebaker Collection.*

Amphibious models were fitted with rear-mounted rudders, a curved bow section, and skirted tracks. Propulsion at sea came via the "water wheel" action of the tracks, with a waterborne top speed of 4 miles per hour.

The Weasel was a Studebaker exclusive, but had the war continued, plans called for Ford to produce them as well.

*Studebaker won the Army-Navy "E" Award for excellence in production in 1944.*

*An amphibious M29C "Weasel" on the assembly line. Note the skirted tracks and stern-mounted rudders.*

*Water-testing the amphibious M29C Weasel in the Louisiana Bayou.*

*One-hundred and eleven Studebaker employees were killed in the line of duty.*

"Lieutenant, corporal and craftsman—the Hinkles still 'work together'"—Tom Hinkle now builds Flying Fortress engines at Studebaker where his record as a motor car craftsman goes back nearly 23 years. At last reports, one son, George, is an Army Air Forces lieutenant in India, Bill Hinkle, Tom's other son, is a Coast Artillery corporal in the Fiji Islands.

## Service

Studebaker's tradition of "Father and Son" craftsmanship took on a new face during World War II. A series of Studebaker advertisements featured fathers at work in the factory while their sons served overseas.

Five thousand six hundred eleven employees served in the armed forces, and Studebaker employees purchased over $26 million in War Bonds during World War II.

One-hundred and eleven Studebaker employees were killed in the line of duty.

STUDEBAKER NATIONAL MUSEUM | 87

## KOREA AND VIETNAM

The Korean War saw Studebaker once again building Army trucks and airplane engines. The engines were now jets, specifically, General Electric J47 jet engines built under license for the B47 Strato-jet.

The jet engines were built at Studebaker-owned factories in New Brunswick, New Jersey, and Chicago, Illinois. Military and civilian truck production took place at the Chippewa Avenue plant.

*Studebaker's first M35-A1 army truck reaches the end of the Chippewa Avenue plant's assembly line in 1962. L-R: Allan Bare, F.D. Durbin, M.H. Hauser, and John Pasalich.*

*J47 jet engine.*

The Chippewa plant was sold in 1956, but repurchased in 1961 in anticipation of additional government contracts. Shortly after the acquisition, Studebaker was tapped to produce 6x6 trucks, this time destined for southeast Asia.

# AM General

When Studebaker closed its South Bend plant in December of 1963, its military contracts and Chippewa Avenue plant were acquired by the Kaiser-Jeep Corporation.

Kaiser-Jeep was purchased by American Motors in 1970, which in turn created the AM General Corporation in 1971 to handle its government contracts.

AM General's corporate headquarters are located in downtown South Bend. Military Hummers and Hummer H2s are built at AM General's plant in neighboring Mishawaka, Indiana.

## 2002 Hummer H2

This was the fifth H2 produced at AM General's Mishawaka, Indiana plant. It is one of several built to test assembly procedures, and was not certified for public sale.

*Engine:* V8, 6.0 liter.

*Horsepower:* 325

*Gift of the AM General Corporation.*

## 1985 HMMWV "Humvee"

The all-terrain High Mobility Multipurpose Wheeled Vehicle (HMMWV) replaced the venerable Army-issue Jeep in 1981. This vehicle is a prototype HMMWV, and features armor plating and a roof-mounted turret.

*Engine:* V8, 6.2 liter Diesel.

*Exhibited through the courtesy of the AM General Corporation.*

# Chapter 7: Limelight

## First By Far...

With no new automobiles available for the duration of World War II, tremendous demand awaited when hostilities ceased in 1945. The industry scrambled to convert its factories back to civilian production, with Ford producing the first postwar automobile on July 3, 1945.

The remaining manufacturers resumed production soon thereafter, each with warmed-over versions of their 1942 models.

*Weasels and M-Series trucks shared production facilities in 1945.*

*Studebaker paymaster Bill Studebaker, son of company founder Henry Studebaker, pilots the first postwar Studebaker automobile off the assembly line.*

Studebaker had other ideas. In the latter stages of the war, Loewy's designers began work on a new postwar automobile. To be the first with a new design in a car-starved market would garner far more publicity than any ad campaign, reasoned Studebaker executives.

As the new Studebakers would not be ready until spring of 1946, production resumed in December of 1945 with a limited run of 1946 Skyway Champions.

*Postwar Champion Mockup, 1943.*

*Paint curing ovens, 1946.*

Like its competitors, the Skyway Champion was a slightly revised version of its 1942 counterpart, but was merely a stopgap until the new models were ready.

"First by Far with a Postwar Car" proclaimed Studebaker advertisements for the new Champions, Commanders, and Land Cruisers.

Studebaker's bold new look debuted in May of 1946 to rave reviews and cemented its reputation as a styling leader.

*1947 Champion.*

*1947 Land Cruiser.*

*Body Assembly, 1947.*

*"First by Far with a Postwar Car."*

Enthusiasm for Studebaker's new automobiles also carried over to the Truck Division. Despite being one of the nation's leading horse-drawn commercial vehicle manufacturers, success in the self-propelled era had proven elusive.

Studebaker addressed this deficiency with the introduction of the M-Series line in 1941. The M-Series set new sales records after the war, retailing nearly 150,000 units before production ended in 1948.

*This is Studebaker's popular half-ton Coupe Express Pick-up—You'll find it an outstanding truck in all-around utility—with the driving comfort and handling ease of a Studebaker passenger car. Studebaker offers a heavy-duty-model truck in several wheel bases too—and the one-ton pick-up shown at top.*

*1941 M5.*

*South Bend's Sollitt Construction Company's M-Series dump truck.*

**STUDEBAKER NATIONAL MUSEUM**

## 1947 M5

Studebaker's M-Series truck line marked Studebaker's first successful entry into the light-duty truck market. The M-Series sourced a number of components from Studebaker's 1941 Champion, including instrument panels, headlight rims, and doors.

Additional savings were realized by making fenders interchangeable front to rear on each side of the truck. Running boards also interchanged side to side.

**Engine:** Inline six-cylinder, 170 cubic inches

**Horsepower:** 70

**Price when new:** $1,082

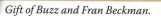
*Gift of Buzz and Fran Beckman.*

*Studebaker's M-Series truck line marked Studebaker's first successful entry into the light-duty truck market.*

The 2R-Series replaced the M-Series for 1949. The 2R-Series was designed by Robert Bourke and built at the company's Chippewa Avenue plant on South Bend's south side. Bourke began work for Raymond Loewy Associates in 1940, and was placed in charge of the Studebaker design studio shortly after World War II.

*Mud-testing Studebaker's "Desert Explorer" version of the 2R-Series. Desert Explorers were built in limited numbers, and specially outfitted for use in arid climates.*

*2R-Series final assembly and inspection.*

*Rugged, handsome and versatile, over a quarter million 2R-Series trucks were built by 1953.*

*2R-Series trucks were available in a wide array of body configurations.*

**STUDEBAKER NATIONAL MUSEUM**

## 1949 Champion

Studebaker's Champion changed very little from 1947 to 1949. The Champion four-door sedan was Studebaker's best seller in 1949, with 24,328 being produced. This Champion features optional fog lights, directional signals, and back-up lights.

*Engine:* Inline six-cylinder, 170 cubic inches
*Horsepower:* 80
*Price when new:* $1,762

*Gift of Mr. Bob Devore.*

# UAW #5

United Auto Workers (UAW) Local #5 was formed in 1935 on a street corner just outside the Studebaker factory. UAW #5 grew to be one of the strongest local unions, providing many benefits and opportunities for its members.

The union organized car pools and rationing during World War II, and later established the Labor-Management Scholarship Fund for members' children. The UAW #5 remains active today, representing workers at AM General's Mishawaka, Indiana, plant.

*Studebaker union activities were stressed at all large employee gatherings. The educational committee for UAW Local #5 arranged this display of posters stressing such services as the union's library, cooperative store, and credit facilities circa 1950.*

*Contract signing, 1952.*

## THE NIFTY FIFTY

Studebaker's iconic "bullet nose" 1950 and 1951 models stemmed from a sketch made by Robert Bourke several years prior. Its aircraft-inspired design was unmistakable, and the "Next Look" Studebakers generated controversy, publicity, and sales.

Studebaker enjoyed a record year with just over 343,000 automobiles produced. Another quarter million bullet-nosed Studebakers were sold in 1951 as sales exceeded $500 million for the first time.

*The "Next Look" Studebakers*

*Hodak Motors, Kankakee, Illinois.*

*The 1950 Studebaker's aircraft-influenced styling is evident in this picture with a US Navy Blue Angels' Grumman F9F Panther.*

While Raymond Loewy's talented troupe of designers handled the aesthetics, Studebaker engineers were hard at work on the mechanics. Automatic transmissions were gaining favor in the late 1940s, and Studebaker jumped into the fray in mid-1950 with its "Automatic Drive" automatic transmission. It was one of the first modern automatic transmissions in the industry, and the first in the low-priced field.

In 1951, Studebaker introduced a new overhead-valve V8 engine in the Commander and Land Cruiser lines. The new V8 offered excellent performance and fuel economy, and proved to be exceptionally rugged and reliable.

*Studebaker's "Automatic Drive" was one of the first modern automatic transmissions in the industry, and the first in the low-priced field.*

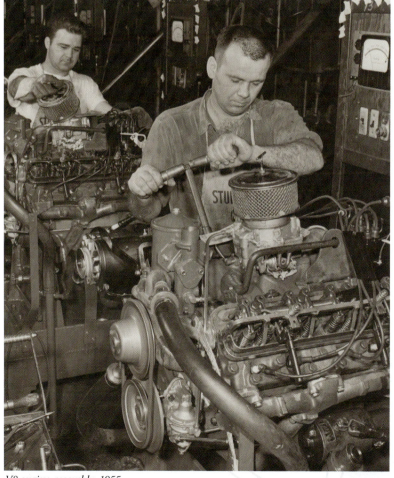

*V8 engine assembly, 1955.*

**STUDEBAKER NATIONAL MUSEUM**

# The Body Drop

The body assembly building at Studebaker's main plant was located at the north side of the complex. Once bodies were complete, they were transported approximately a quarter mile away to the final assembly building located on the plant's south end.

*Body drop, 1953.*

*Body drop, 1952.*

It was during final assembly that the body drop took place. The car bodies were "dropped" through a hole in the third floor onto the appropriate chassis moving along the second floor. The whole process was synchronized so all components arrived at the proper time.

*During Studebaker's Centennial Celebration in 1952, the company tracked the production of the last car of Studebaker's first century and the first car of Studebaker's second century. In this image, the bodies belonging to both cars are being trucked to final assembly on February 17, 1952.*

*The car bodies were "dropped" through a hole in the third floor onto the appropriate chassis moving along the second floor.*

*The Studebaker National Museum's "Body Drop" display is found in the AM General Atrium.*

**STUDEBAKER NATIONAL MUSEUM**

## 1950 Commander Starlight Coupe

This Starlight Coupe was produced at Studebaker's Los Angeles, California, plant. Studebaker produced vehicles in California from 1936-1956.

Like many cars of this vintage destined for warm climates, it is not equipped with a heater, but does feature Studebaker's new-for-1950 "Automatic Drive" automatic transmission.

*Engine:* Inline six-cylinder, 245 cubic inches.

*Horsepower:* 102

*Price when new:* $2,018

*Gift of the estate of Mr. Milton Kroah.*

*Like many cars of this vintage destined for warm climates, it is not equipped with a heater.*

*Presenting*
*the newest and most advanced automatic transmission*

# STUDEBAKER
## *Automatic Drive*

**No clutch pedal, of course!** But there's nothing new to learn. You just drive in the usual way—without any clutching, declutching or shifting gears. Marvelous for "new" drivers.

STUDEBAKER engineers once again have worked their magic on the mechanism of the modern automobile!

Together with Borg-Warner engineers they have perfected—and proudly present—America's newest and most advanced "no clutch—no gearshift" driving.

This revolutionary Studebaker Automatic Drive takes over much of the physical effort of driving a car.

It's a combination of torque converter and direct mechanical drive—brilliant triumph of nearly 15 years' research by the most exacting technicians in the automotive industry!

Try out Studebaker's new Automatic Drive without obligation. It's extra cost—but it's the finest investment that anybody ever made in motoring enjoyment.

**You simply set this selector lever!** All you do is feed the gas. The new Studebaker Automatic Drive does the rest by "shifting for itself"—in traffic slow-downs and everywhere.

# 1951 Commander

This car was used during the filming of "The Muppet Movie" in 1979. The car was specially rigged to allow it to be driven from the trunk, as it was used for close-up "driving" shots of Fozzie Bear and Kermit the Frog.

*Gift of the Studebaker Drivers Club-Orange Empire Chapter in care of Richard and Phyllis Holcomb.*

The person driving the car navigated by means of a television monitor fed by a camera located in the "bullet" hole up front. Poster paint was used to prepare the car for filming. It is cheaper to apply and photographs better than automobile paint, but deteriorates very quickly. After production wrapped, the car was sold by the studio and spent many years in outdoor storage.

*Engine:* V8, 232 cubic inches.

*Horsepower:* 120

*Price when new:* $1,997

*The car was rigged to be driven from the trunk. The driver had to lie almost on his or her back, as the pedals were located at the top of the trunk compartment.*

# CENTENNIAL

The year 1952 marked Studebaker's centennial, and the company embarked on a year-long celebration to commemorate the occasion. The Indianapolis 500 selected a Studebaker Commander convertible to serve as Pace Car for that year's race. Prior to the race, Studebaker staged a "Parade of Transportation" at the speedway featuring nearly every vehicle in its collection.

Studebaker spent $500,000 to produce three short motion pictures celebrating its history, and the South Bend Tribune published a 132-page special edition commemorating Studebaker's 100 years.

*Dwight Eisenhower visits South Bend during a campaign stop in 1952. Seated in the passenger seat is the Hon. Robert Grant, Ike's Indiana campaign manager.*

*Centennial medallions were distributed to each Studebaker employee. The medallions were designed by John Ebstein of Raymond Loewy Associates.*

*Quarter-scale model of the 1952 Commander Starliner Hardtop.*

*A 1952 Studebaker Commander served as Pace Car for the 1952 Indianapolis 500.*

**STUDEBAKER NATIONAL MUSEUM**

## THE MARY-ANN CLUB

On January 14, 1910, Miss Bertha M. Nixon and 23 other women formed a social club for Studebaker's female employees. The Mary-Ann Club became one of South Bend's most prestigious social and service organizations with membership exceeding 500 women at its peak.

The club took its name in honor of J.M. Studebaker's wife Mary and Clement's wife Ann. The group met every other week, and hosted a number of activities ranging from hay rides to stage plays.

The club chartered the Studebaker Girls' Glee Club (later known as the Harmonettes) in 1937, and a west coast branch of the Mary-Ann Club was organized at Studebaker's Los Angeles factory that same year.

*The Harmonettes c. 1950.*

*Trudy Joswiak, Rosa Hahn, and Carol Zesinger pose in costume for the Mary-Ann Club's 1950 Buccaneer Ball.*

The Mary-Ann Club held its first banquet in 1914, and began to emphasize charity work as one of its purposes. Members distributed food and gifts to the less fortunate families of the community, and made personal visits to those in poor health.

Many South Bend area organizations benefited from the Mary-Ann Club's over fifty years of hard work including Damon Runyan Cancer Fund, South Bend's Logan Center, Memorial Hospital, St. Joseph Hospital, Camp Eberhart, Camp Millhouse, and the Northern Indiana Children's Hospital.

The Mary-Ann Club presented the "Century of Fashions Parade" as part of their spring banquet held May 15, 1952. L-R: Pat Kovatch, Rosalie Welsh, Jean Kirkpatrick, Pat Klute, Virginia Moritz, Dororthy Rogowski, Natalie Toth, Bea Knoll, and Lillian Bokon.

*Naval Trainees were admitted free to the Mary-Ann Club Dance held on October 21, 1944.*

*Many South Bend area organizations benefited from the Mary-Ann Club's over fifty years of hard work.*

STUDEBAKER NATIONAL MUSEUM

# 1952 Commander Starliner Hardtop

Studebaker introduced the popular hardtop body style in 1952 in both the Commander and Champion lines. The body style was formally known as a "Hardtop Convertible" and designed to combine the openness of a convertible with the protection of a steel roof.

Just under 25,000 Starliner Hardtops were built in 1952.

**Engine:** V8, 232 cubic inches.
**Horsepower:** 120
**Price when new:** $2,448

*Gift of Thomas J. and Charlotte Hansen, and R.W. and Joan Thornton.*

*The Hardtop body style echoed the Duplex Phaeton of 1925-1926.*

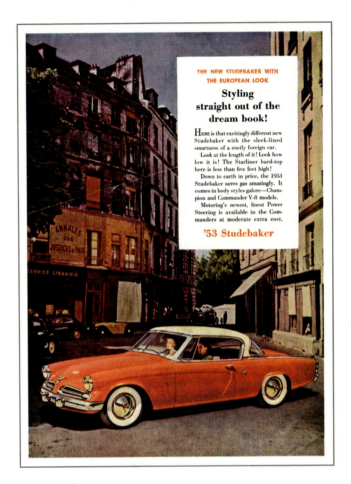

*Design sketch for the 1953 Starliner.*

*1953 Commander Starliner.*

## The Masterpiece

The stunning 1953 Studebaker coupes and hardtops trace their roots to late 1951 when Robert Bourke was given the go-ahead to create a special show car. While many show cars are created as a singular work of art, Bourke decided this project would keep production realities firmly in mind.

Upon its completion, a showing was scheduled with Studebaker's Board of Directors, and the following morning Bourke received word that his show car was slated for production. The 1953 Studebaker Starliner would win a dozen awards for design excellence, and is considered by many as Studebaker's masterpiece.

## 1953 Champion Starliner

The 1953 Studebaker Starliner was available in both the Champion and Commander lines. The streamlined Starliner stood in stark contrast to the competition's upright and perpendicular design themes, and sat a full six inches lower than its peers.

Early 1953 Studebakers featured a 'tri-star' trim motif, but this was removed mid-year due to objections from Mercedes-Benz.

*Engine:* Inline six-cylinder, 170 cubic inches.

**Horsepower:** 90

*Price when new:* $2,116

*Gift of Mr. Warren Reinecker.*

*The streamlined Starliner stood in stark contrast to the competition's upright and perpendicular design themes...*

*Final Assembly, 1953.*

The immediate postwar era was Studebaker's most prosperous. Bolstered by a strong seller's market, the 100 year-old Studebaker Corporation established itself as a styling leader and enjoyed record-setting years in both sales and production.

However, the seller's market was subsiding, and lingering below the surface lay significant problems that would haunt the venerable company as the 1950s progressed.

*The new Studebaker-Packard Corporation was introduced at the company's "Preview Rally" held at Notre Dame Stadium September 26, 1954. The new 1955 models were shown to the public followed by a program featuring Bob Hope, Les Brown, and other notables.*

The Studebaker Corporation was not a small company; it usually ranked as one of the top 75 American corporations. Studebaker's main competition, namely Ford, General Motors, and Chrysler, were three of the nation's largest. As the decade progressed, Studebaker found it increasingly difficult to compete with the "Big 3."

In addition to the economies of scale, Studebaker was beset by other problems. Studebaker paid the highest wages in the industry in 1953, and had done so since the end of the war. While other manufacturers endured strikes after World War II to stabilize labor costs, Studebaker did not. This kept the lines moving in the high-demand postwar era, but merely deferred the issue until later.

*The Studebaker plant c. 1950.*

Production problems with Studebaker's new Starliner Hardtop and Starlight Coupe hampered the company out of the gate in 1953. A strike at Studebaker's transmission supplier later that year slowed assembly lines even further.

In 1954, Ford and Chevrolet staged a heated sales war. Ford and Chevy dealers were flooded with cars with orders to sell them or else. The resulting price war was felt by the entire industry, and Studebaker posted a $26 million loss for 1954.

*1954 Champion Starliner.*

*Final assembly, 1955.*

## Packard

On June 22, 1954, the Studebaker Corporation merged with the Packard Motor Car Company. Detroit-based Packard was once America's foremost luxury automobile manufacturer, and sought to reestablish itself in that field.

On paper, the partnership made sense — the new Studebaker-Packard Corporation now offered automobiles in every price class, as well as a full line of commercial vehicles.

In reality, neither company was healthy. Studebaker's red ink was partially offset by Packard's influx of cash, but Studebaker's high labor costs remained, as did Packard's production woes at its Conner Avenue plant in Detroit.

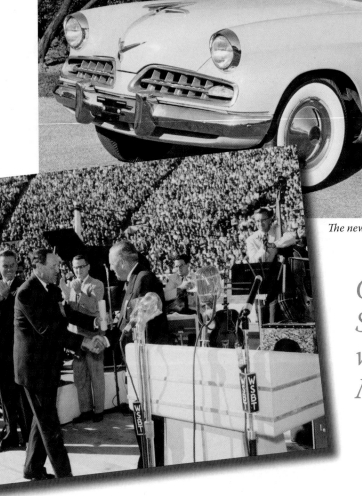

*The new-for-1954 Studebaker Conestoga station wagon.*

*Paul Hoffman welcomes new Studebaker-Packard President James Nance at the 1955 Preview Party held at Notre Dame Stadium on September 26, 1954.*

*On June 22, 1954 Studebaker merged with the Packard Motor Car Company.*

# 1956 Packard Predictor

The Packard Predictor was created for the 1956 Auto Show circuit by Packard designer Richard Teague. The Predictor was based on the Clipper chassis and built by Italian coach builder Ghia in just 90 days. The Predictor features a retractable rear window, roll top roof panels, and swiveling seats for easy entry.

*From the original Studebaker Collection.*

*The Packard Predictor at the Chicago Auto Show.*

STUDEBAKER NATIONAL MUSEUM

## Studebaker-Packard

The new Studebaker-Packard Corporation quickly took action. Studebaker's sedan line abandoned the streamlined "Loewy look" for 1956 in favor of a more conventional appearance. Studebaker's Hawk line, led by the potent Golden Hawk, also debuted in 1956 and was marketed as a "family sports car." The no-frills Scotsman appeared in mid-1957, and sold for an industry-low $1,776.

*1957 Golden Hawk.*

*University of Notre Dame Tennis Team members admire the new 1956 President.*

*1957 Scotsman station wagon.*

*Gift of Mr. William Seidel.*

## 1957 Golden Hawk 400

Studebaker Golden Hawks were among the fastest automobiles on the road in the late 1950s. The ultra-luxurious Golden Hawk "400" was introduced in the spring of 1957, and featured hand-buffed leather interior and special paint.

This Golden Hawk is the first of the 41 Golden Hawk "400s" produced.

*Engine:* V8, 289 cubic inches, supercharged.
*Horsepower:* 275
*Price when new:* $4,208

STUDEBAKER NATIONAL MUSEUM | 121

### 1958 Scotsman

The Scotsman debuted in mid-1957 as Studebaker's entry-level model. Intended strictly as "basic transportation," the Scotsman was a Studebaker Champion devoid of all trim and accessories.

Customers were limited to three color choices and an extremely limited option list. Yet, the Scotsman proved to be a success, with over 20,000 produced during its year and a half run.

*Engine:* Inline six-cylinder, 185 cubic inches.

*Horsepower:* 101

*Price when new:* $1,776

*Gift of Mr. Andy Krizman.*

## THE LARK

Despite the relative success of the Hawk and the Scotsman, only 54,000 1958 Studebakers were sold, compared to nearly 350,000 eight years earlier. Collectively, Studebaker-Packard failed to show a profit in any year since the 1954 merger.

Following the 1958 model year, the Packard line was discontinued and Studebaker's future lay in the hands of Studebaker-Packard President Harold Churchill and the new 1959 Lark.

*Water-testing the 1959 Lark.*

*Collectively, Studebaker-Packard failed to show a profit in any year since the 1954 merger.*

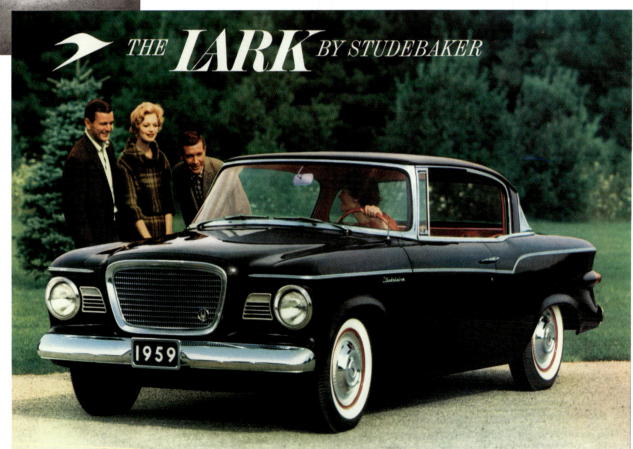

The success of the Scotsman and increasing sales of imported cars led Churchill to conclude that an untapped market existed for an economical family car.

Larger than foreign cars, yet smaller than domestic competitors, the Lark captured the spirit of Studebaker's 1939 Champion, offering a well-built economical automobile without sacrificing comfort or roominess. Sales tripled over the year before, and Studebaker recorded a profit for the first time since 1953.

*The Lark four-door station wagon was new for 1960.*

*Eli Spicer, of South Bend's Freeman-Spicer dealership, sends off his daughter Susie Spicer (left) and Mira Satori in a 1960 Lark Convertible. Mr. Spicer is a Life Trustee of the Studebaker National Museum.*

# BONNIE DOON'S

Every community had its favorite drive-in, and South Bend's was Bonnie Doon's. In 1938 Herman and Andrew Muldoon opened the first Bonnie Doon's drive-in. Other locations soon sprang up across the area.

The Bonnie Doon's drive-in on South Bend's South Michigan Street was one stop on the unofficial "Merry Go 'Round" cruise route that also included Azar's Big Boy. A Bonnie Doon's restaurant, complete with carhop service, remains on Lincolnway East in Mishawaka, Indiana.

*Bonnie Doon's fleet of four Studebakers and one Packard, 1956. Bonnie Doon's purchased numerous Studebaker cars and trucks for use as company vehicles.*

*The Studebaker National Museum's Upper Level Gallery features a re-created Bonnie Doon's drive-in.*

# SHERWOOD EGBERT

The 1960 model year greeted Studebaker with new compacts from Ford, General Motors, and Chrysler. Facing head-to-head competition with the "Big 3," Studebaker again lost money in 1960.

Sluggish sales of Studebaker's 1961 models led the Studebaker board to replace President Harold Churchill. Sherwood Egbert, formerly of the McCulloch Corporation, took office on February 1, 1961.

*Studebaker sponsored the "Mr. Ed" television program from 1961-1963.
L-R: Bamboo Harvester (Mr. Ed), Alan Young (Wilbur Post), Connie Hines (Carol Post).*

*1961 Lark.*

*Gift of Mr. John Brichetto.*

## 1961 Champ

Studebaker introduced the Champ truck in 1960. The Champ was based heavily on the Lark, and harkened back to the Coupe Express of the 1930s.

Many Lark components were used in the cab body and interior, and the Champ momentarily rejuvenated Studebaker's flagging truck division. The Champ remained in production until the closing of Studebaker's South Bend plant in December of 1963.

*Engine:* Inline six-cylinder, 170 cubic inches.

*Horsepower:* 112

*Price when new:* $1,811

*Body drop on the Champ assembly line, 1962.*

**STUDEBAKER NATIONAL MUSEUM** | 127

## 1961 Hawk

Studebaker's Hawk line consisted of just one model in 1961, and was called simply the "Hawk." Production was to be limited to 6,100 vehicles, which Studebaker was in no danger of reaching given it had only produced 3,800 Hawks in 1960.

New features for 1961 included semi-bucket seats and a four-speed transmission. This Hawk is finished in "Flamingo" a color exclusive to the Hawk and Lark convertible.

*Engine:* V8, 289 cubic inches

*Horsepower:* 225

*Price when new:* $2,650

*Gift of a Friend of the Studebaker National Museum.*

Unlike his recent predecessors, Sherwood Egbert was not a Studebaker veteran, nor did he have previous experience in the automobile industry. After a brief survey of the situation, Egbert determined Studebaker needed a vigorous image overhaul.

In late February 1961, Egbert commissioned Raymond Loewy, who last worked for Studebaker in 1955, to design a new sports car. He also tapped Brooks Stevens to update the Hawk and the Lark.

*Sherwood Egbert*

*1962 Gran Tursimo Hawk*

*Studebaker paced the Indianapolis 500 for the fourth and final time in 1962. L-R: Indianapolis, Indiana, Studebaker dealer Charlie Stuart, Indianapolis Motor Speedway owner Tony Hulman, Sherwood Egbert.*

**STUDEBAKER NATIONAL MUSEUM** | 129

## The Avanti

After meeting with Egbert, Loewy assembled his team and sequestered them at a Palm Springs, California, bungalow. For the next six weeks they worked around the clock creating the Studebaker Avanti.

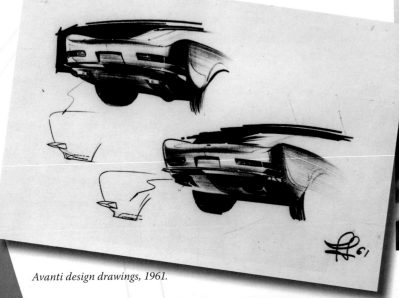

*Avanti design drawings, 1961.*

*Raymond Loewy's Avanti design team (L-R): Tom Kellogg, Raymond Loewy, Bob Andrews, and John Ebstein.*

*Avanti production line, 1963.*

Once completed, the design arrived in South Bend and the company worked feverishly to prepare the Avanti for production. Normal industry time frames dictate three to five years for this process.

The Avanti debuted fourteen months later at the 1962 Indianapolis 500. Studebaker's new fiberglass-bodied high performance Avanti was billed as "America's Most Advanced Automobile." It retailed for $4,445.

The Avanti was met with a surge of publicity and orders upon its introduction, but problems at Studebaker's body supplier slowed production to a trickle. Hindered by the slow start, the Avanti never regained its initial momentum.

*Sherwood Egbert and Studebaker Vice-President Nello Lamberti pose in front of a shipment of Avantis.*

*Avanti interior.*

*Publicity photo of the Studebaker Avanti. Raymond Loewy is standing in the background on the right.*

**STUDEBAKER NATIONAL MUSEUM**

## 1962 Sedan Prototype

In 1962, Studebaker President Sherwood Egbert instructed designer Brooks Stevens to submit designs for future Studebaker automobiles. One of Stevens's designs included this sedan prototype planned for 1965.

The car features a one piece hood-fender stamping and diagonally interchangeable doors. The Brooks Stevens prototypes were built by coachbuilder Sibona-Bassano in Turin, Italy.

**Cost to build:** $16,500

*Gift of the Studebaker Drivers Club, the Lyon Foundation, and Kay and Ron Radecki.*

*Brooks Stevens previous designs included the Lawn Boy lawnmower and the Oscar Meyer Wienermobile.*

*"Sibona-Bassano" badges are located on the front fenders.*

*Gift of the Studebaker Drivers Club, the Lyon Foundation, and Kay and Ron Radecki.*

# 1962 Skyview

Brooks Stevens' Skyview station wagon was slated for 1964, and featured the rear sliding roof panel found on Studebaker's Wagonaire. It also shared the Wagonaire's high-mounted taillights.

Like the sedan prototype, the doors were diagonally interchangeable, and the bumpers were the same front and rear.

*Cost to build:* $16,500

*Studebaker's 1963-1966 Wagonaire shared the Skyview's sliding roof feature.*

STUDEBAKER NATIONAL MUSEUM | 133

## 1962 Sceptre

The Sceptre was intended to replace the Hawk in 1966. The headlight is a single tubular unit developed by Sylvania. It was designed to distribute light more evenly, while minimizing glare to oncoming traffic. The "C" pillars are translucent polarized glass, and the interior features an upright "console" instrument panel.

Studebaker's financial position precluded further development of Stevens' prototypes. Stevens retained the three vehicles and displayed them at his Mequon, Wisconsin, museum until his death in 1995.

**Cost to build:** $16,500

*Gift of the Studebaker Drivers Club, the Lyon Foundation, and Kay and Ron Radecki.*

*Final assembly, fall of 1963.*

## BLACK MONDAY

By 1963, Studebaker's financial position was as grim as it was in 1958, and the board was seriously considering liquidating the automobile division. Just as in 1958, Studebaker's fate rested with the success or failure of its new models.

The 1964 line featured crisp new styling by Brooks Stevens paired with an emphasis on performance. In October of 1963, a fleet of 1964 Studebakers led by Andy Granatelli captured a total of 339 United States Auto Club (USAC) speed and endurance records at the Bonneville Salt Flats.

*1964 Daytona Convertible.*

*Andy Granatelli.*

*Andy Granatelli captured a total of 339 United States Auto Club (USAC) speed and endurance records.*

**STUDEBAKER NATIONAL MUSEUM**

# 1964 Pursuit Marshal

Studebaker actively sought fleet sales in the 1950s and 1960s, and created several heavy duty models intended for police and taxi use. The Marshal was Studebaker's police model, and was available in three versions, the City Marshal, the Patrol Marshal, and the Pursuit Marshal.

The Pursuit Marshal was Studebaker's high-performance interceptor model, and featured many of the Avanti's high-performance components.

*Engine:* V8, 289 cubic inches.

*Horsepower:* 240

*Gift of Gladys Christian in memory of Jack Merrill.*

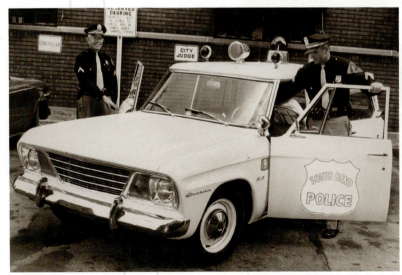

*South Bend police officers Jim Hertel and Don Cornelis prepare to head out on patrol.*

*The South Bend Police Department's fleet of 1942 Studebaker Champions.*

Despite Studebaker's best efforts, sales did not improve. On December 9, 1963, Studebaker announced it was closing the South Bend plant and cancelling the Gran Turismo Hawk, Avanti, and all truck production. All remaining models would be sourced from Studebaker's Hamilton, Ontario factory.

*Studebaker's Gate #1, December 20, 1963.*

## 1964 Daytona Hardtop

The last regular-production South Bend-built Studebaker was produced on December 20, 1963, and was originally destined for Pennsylvania.

Studebaker substituted another car for the Pennsylvania customer and retained this car for its vehicle collection. It shows less than 50 miles on the odometer.

*Engine:* V8, 289 cubic inches.

*Horsepower:* 240

*Price when new:* $2,635.83

*From the original Studebaker Collection.*

*The last regular-production South Bend-built Studebaker was destined for Boyer Brothers Studebaker in Moselem Springs, Pennsylvania.*

# Canada

Studebaker's history in Canada dates to 1910, when the company established Studebaker of Canada, Ltd., with a factory in Walkerville, Ontario.

The Walkerville plant closed in 1936, leaving Studebaker without a Canadian plant until it purchased the former Rofors anti-aircraft gun factory in Hamilton, Ontario in 1946.

*First shipment of Canadian Studebakers to United States.*

*Studebaker's Hamilton, Ontario plant stands in the background as 1964 Studebakers are loaded for shipping.*

Despite producing a plant record 19,435 automobiles in 1965, the Studebaker Corporation discontinued automobile production midway through the 1966 model year.

Though the corporation continued to exist through its subsidiary divisions such as STP and Onan Generator, its 114-year tradition of vehicle manufacturing had come to an end.

*The first 1965 Studebaker. L-R: Director of Manufacuturing W.A Moeser, Studebaker Automotive Sales Corporation (SASCO) President Gordon Grundy.*

Studebaker telegrammed its dealers on March 4, 1966, to announce it was permanently leaving the automobile business.

On March 17, 1966, at 8:11 a.m., the last Studebaker rolled off the Hamilton assembly line.

*The Studebaker Corporation telegrammed its dealers on March 4, 1966 to announce it was permanently leaving the automobile business.*

*1966 Daytona Sports Sedan.*

### 1966 Cruiser

On Thursday, March 17, at 8:11 a.m., the last Studebaker, a 1966 Cruiser finished in Timberline Turquoise, left the Hamilton, Ontario, factory. The car was largely completed on the 16th, but was left at the end of the line as the media was scheduled to arrive the following morning.

As the car was being built, workers "personalized' certain areas with their names and initials, most of which remain visible today. Unlike other historically significant Studebaker vehicles, the last Studebaker saw regular service as a company vehicle before it was placed in the collection in 1969.

*Engine:* V8, 283 cubic inches

*Horsepower:* 195

*Price when new:* $2,405

*From the original Studebaker Collection.*

*Mr. Budnayk etched his name into the cowl.*

# Chapter 9: Legacy

"This is not Studebaker, Indiana, this is South Bend, Indiana!" proclaimed local businessman Paul Gilbert at a press conference following Studebaker's closing. "And, ladies and gentlemen, before we get through here, I think we're going to have to pray harder and work harder!"

Indeed, Studebaker was the city's largest employer, and nearly 7,000 people were out of work after the shutdown.

The city reacted quickly to the crisis with an outpouring of support. Indiana's legislators secured federal aid to re-train workers, and by 1966, South Bend's unemployment rate had fallen below pre-closing levels.

*Studebaker building 78, 1926.*

## "This is not Studebaker, Indiana, this is South Bend, Indiana!"

*Studebaker building 78, just prior to its demolition in 2006.*

## THE AVANTI II

South Bend Studebaker dealers Leo Newman and Nate Altman were unhappy with Studebaker's decision to discontinue the Avanti in December of 1963. Newman and Altman felt strongly that the Avanti deserved a second chance, and approached nearly every American automobile manufacturer about adopting the car. When no takers were found, Newman and Altman formed the Avanti Motors Corporation and acquired all the necessary equipment, parts and facilities to produce the car.

The Avanti II was built in a section of the former Studebaker plant by many veteran Studebaker employees. Production was limited to several hundred per year, as each Avanti II built by hand to the customer's order. The Avanti II was built in South Bend until 1987, at which time production moved to Ohio, and later to Georgia. An updated version of the Avanti penned by original design team member Tom Kellogg debuted in 1998.

STUDEBAKER NATIONAL MUSEUM | 145

### 1975 Avanti II

This Avanti II was owned by Raymond Loewy and was kept at his estate in France. To comply with French traffic laws, the car was fitted with additional rear driving lights. The car features some of Loewy's personal touches, such as the white stripe on each door, and the gold "S" insert in the hood ornament. The gold "S" was used on early Studebaker Avantis, but not on Avanti IIs.

*Engine:* V8, 350 cubic inches
*Horsepower:* 220
*Price when new:* $8,705

*Exhibited through the courtesy of Laurence Loewy.*

The "S" medallion was nicknamed the "Pirate's Buckle" by Studebaker designers. It was not fitted to Avanti IIs, but was added to this car by Raymond Loewy.

## TIPPECANOE PLACE

In 1886, Clement Studebaker commissioned architect Henry Ives Cobb to design his new home. Tippecanoe Place was completed in 1889 at a cost of $250,000, and featured forty rooms and twenty fireplaces. Clement Studebaker resided at Tippecanoe until his death in 1901, with the rest of the family remaining until 1933.

Tippecanoe's later tenants included the American Red Cross and a school for handicapped children. Today, Tippecanoe Place is one of South Bend's finest restaurants. It is located just east of the Studebaker National Museum on Washington Street.

*The Drawing Room at Tippecanoe Place as it originally appeared.*

## Philanthropy

The Studebakers were among South Bend's wealthiest families and made many contributions for the betterment of their community.

In 1897 Clement and Anne Studebaker donated $150,000 in land and capital for an expansion of Epworth (now Memorial) Hospital. Concerned over a lack of commercial office space in downtown South Bend, J.M. Studebaker financed construction of the JMS Building in the early 1900s.

*The JMS Building is located at the corner of Main and Washington Streets in downtown South Bend.*

*St. Paul's Memorial United Methodist Church was founded by Clement Studebaker. It is located at Colfax and LaPorte Avenues in South Bend.*

No fewer than four churches were built due to the Studebakers' generosity, and South Bend's first YMCA was underwritten by J.M. Studebaker in memory of his brothers.

In the early 1920s, Studebaker President Albert Erskine gave a large parcel of land to the City of South Bend for creation of a park. The land became Erskine Golf Course, and remains the largest single gift ever received by the city.

*South Bend's first YMCA was located at the corner of Main and Wayne Streets in downtown South Bend.*

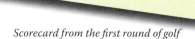

*Scorecard from the first round of golf played at Erskine Golf Course.*

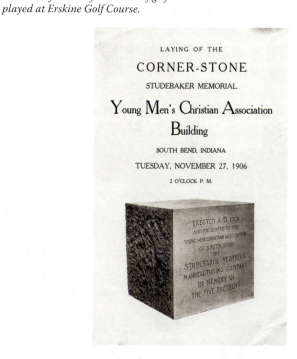

## FAMILIES OF CRAFTSMEN

As a corporate citizen for over 100 years, Studebaker played a significant role in South Bend's cultural history. Employee recruitment in the United States and overseas brought many new families to the area and entire neighborhoods of Studebaker employees sprang up across South Bend.

Studebaker offered "Learn English" classes in the early 20th century, and also offered courses in "Office Training." Studebaker employees also had many extra-curricular activities available. In addition to the Mary-Ann Club (see pages 108-109), Studebaker men and women could participate in athletic team sports, hobby clubs, and musical groups.

*The Studebaker baseball team, 1916.*

*Entire neighborhoods of Studebaker employees sprang up across South Bend.*

*Studebaker's 1927 league champion basketball team.*

*Eight members of the Wilk family were proud Studebaker employees.*

*"Learn English" posting in English, Polish and Hungarian.*

STUDEBAKER NATIONAL MUSEUM | 151

## THE CLUBS

Studebaker's legacy endures on an international scale due in large part to the hard work and dedication of the Studebaker Drivers Club (SDC), the Antique Studebaker Club (ASC), and the Avanti Owners Association International (AOAI).

Harry Barnes founded the SDC in 1962 with the Studebaker Corporation's blessing. Today the SDC boasts over 12,000 members on six continents. The ASC was formed in 1970, and is devoted exclusively to pre-1947 Studebaker cars and trucks. The AOAI was chartered in 1966, and is dedicated to the preservation and operation of Studebaker and post-Studebaker Avantis.

*Members of the Studebaker Drivers Club, Antique Studebaker Club, and Avanti Owners Association toured the former Studebaker Proving Ground's three-mile oval test track during the 2007 Studebaker Drivers Club International Meet.*

*Studebaker's legacy endures on an international scale.*

# Chapter 10: The Collection

*The Studebaker National Museum's "living sign" is located on the museum's east side and pays tribute to the Studebaker Proving Ground's tree sign (see page 48).*

# History of the Studebaker National Museum

The Studebaker National Museum traces its roots to Clement Studebaker's purchase of the Lincoln and Lafayette carriages in the late 1880s. These carriages were soon joined by other significant Studebaker vehicles and artifacts in the Studebaker Brothers Manufacturing Company's private collection.

The collection was placed on display at Studebaker's Administration Building upon its completion in 1909. The Studebaker Corporation continued to collect and display vehicles until automobile production ended in March of 1966.

*The original Studebaker Museum resided on the main floor of Studebaker's Administration Building.*

Later that year, the 37-unit collection and company archives were given to the city of South Bend. The agreement stipulated that the city provide a "suitable home" to house and display the vehicles. The collection had several different homes during the next forty years, including the former Studebaker Administration Building and South Bend's Century Center convention center.

The Museum moved into the former Freeman-Spicer Studebaker dealership in 1983. The Freeman-Spicer building served well as the Museum's home for the next 23 years, but increasing structural and environmental issues dictated the need for a new facility. Planning began in 2003 on a brand-new 55,000 square foot structure.

*The museum's main exhibit gallery at the former Freeman-Spicer Studebaker dealership.*

The new Studebaker National Museum would be built in partnership with the City of South Bend, and be located adjacent to the Center for History, St. Joseph County's history museum.

*The collection was displayed as part of the Discovery Hall Museum at South Bend's Century Center.*

## The New Museum

On October 28, 2005, the Studebaker National Museum unveiled its new building. Over a thousand visitors toured the museum during its inaugural weekend of grand opening festivities.

Visitors to the museum enter via the AM General Atrium. The Atrium showcases the museum's "Body Drop" display and is also a popular location for special events and facility rentals.

At the east end of the AM General Atrium is the Carmichael Bullet Nose Gallery, which features a selected Studebaker on a revolving turntable and street-level showroom windows.

The Studebaker National Museum Grand Opening, October 28, 2005. L-R: South Bend Mayor Steve Luecke, Center for History President Brian Harding, Rev. Leonard F. Chrobot, Indiana Speaker of the House B. Patrick Bauer, Studebaker National Museum President Mark McDonnell, Studebaker Drivers Club President Ed Reynolds, South Bend Councilwoman Charlotte Pfeiffer, and South Bend Heritage Foundation President Tom Miller.

The new Studebaker National Museum.

The Carmichael Bullet Nose Gallery.

*Main Level Gallery*

The Studebaker National Museum features approximately 70 vehicles on interpreted display at any one time, plus an additional 30 in "Visible Storage" in the museum's Lower Level Gallery. In "Visible Storage," vehicles not currently on exhibit are housed in two-tiered racking, and can be seen by everyday museum goers. The collection is also home to artifacts from area industries, such as the South Bend Bait Co., South Bend Lathe, South Bend Toy Co., and Wheelhorse Tractor.

Visitors begin their tour in the Main Level Gallery. This space is home to the 1st Source Bank Presidential Collection which features the museum's presidential vehicles and artifacts. The Upper Level Gallery is home to the S. Ray and Linda Miller Special Exhibition Area. The Studebaker National Museum presents two major special exhibits annually. Past exhibits have featured alternative-fuel vehicles, Indiana-built automobiles, and muscle cars.

Each spring, the Studebaker National Museum recognizes those who have given "more than they promised" at its annual Hall of Champions Dinner. The Hall of Champions' first inductee was Andy Granatelli in 2002, and the event has grown to become one of South Bend's premier evenings.

*Visible Storage*

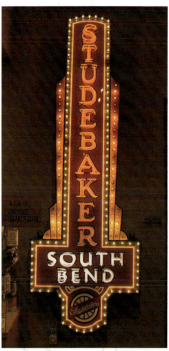
*This Studebaker dealer sign is an exact replica of those used in the 1920s. Gift of the Antique Studebaker Club.*

**STUDEBAKER NATIONAL MUSEUM**

# The Archives

In addition to the vehicle collection, the Studebaker National Museum holds the surviving archives of the Studebaker Corporation and the Packard Motor Car Company.

The 70-ton collection dates to 1853, and its primary holdings include an image collection with over 50,000 images, company publications, sales literature, dealer and production records, and engineering drawings.

The Archives has had several homes since 1966. Following Studebaker's closing, the vast collection resided at Syracuse University until 1977. That year, the archives returned to South Bend and moved several more times over the next three decades.

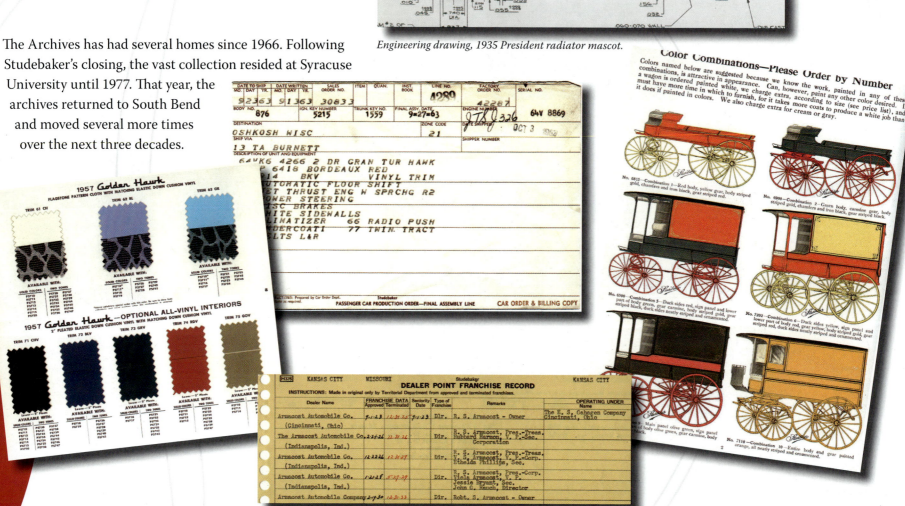

*Engineering drawing, 1935 President radiator mascot.*

When planning began for the new museum building, Studebaker National Museum Trustees began investigating a new location for the archives. In 2005, the Indiana Department of Transportation greenlighted a federally funded project to renovate a 19th-century commercial building into the new Studebaker National Museum Archives.

The building was previously occupied by a grocery store and several taverns, and is located just across the street from the museum. The project was completed in October of 2007.

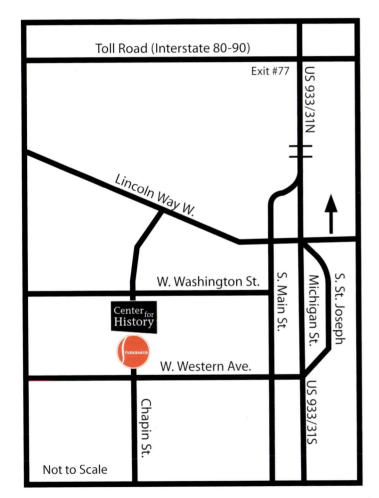

*Studebaker National Museum Archives.*

The new Studebaker National Museum Archives features fully climate-controlled storage areas and a research room open to the public.

The Studebaker National Museum can be found on the internet at studebakermuseum.org.

*studebakermuseum.org*

201 S. Chapin Street, South Bend, IN 46601 (574) 235-9714

## THE VEHICLES
1863 Hearse 11
1904 Model C 30
1912 Flanders 20 32
1913 Model 25 33
1916 Four-Forty Roadster 37
1917 Water Cart 81
1919 Izzer Buggy 39
1919 Big Six 38
1920 Farm Wagon 40
1920 Light Six 44
1924 Light Six 45
1926 Big Six Duplex Phaeton 46
1927 Commander Sedan 52
1927 President Limousine 47
1928 Commander Roadster 54
1928 Studebaker Fire Truck 56
1931 Studebaker Six Roadster 57
1932 President Convertible Coupe 61
1934 Bendix SWC 67
1935 Commander Roadster 69
1937 Coupe Express 72
1947 M5 96
1949 Champion 98
1950 Commander Starlight Coupe 104
1951 Commander 106
1952 Commander Starliner Hardtop 110
1953 Champion Starliner 112
1956 Packard Predictor 119
1957 Golden Hawk 400 121
1958 Scotsman 122
1961 Champ 127
1961 Hawk 128
1962 Skyview 133
1962 Sceptre 134
1962 Sedan Prototype 132
1964 Daytona Hardtop 138
1964 Pursuit Marshal 136
1966 Cruiser 142
1975 Avanti II 146
1985 HMMWV HUMVEE 90
2002 Hummer H2 90
Backward-Forward Car 31
Centennial Wagon 21
Columbian Exposition Wagon 22
Conestoga Wagon 7, 8
Grant's Landau 19
Harrison's Brougham 20
Lafayette Carriage 18
Lincoln Carriage 16

### A
Aldrich, Jake 74
Alhroth, Frank 74
Allen, Woodson 46
Altman, Nate 145
AM General 89
Andrews, Bob 130
Antique Studebaker Club (ASC) 152
Arnold, Mike 57
Ashland, Ohio 6
Associated Transit Company 38
Atalanta Radiator Mascot 47
Atlantic City, New Jersey 54
Auman, Paul 49
Avanti 137
Avanti II 145, 146
Avanti Motors 145
Avanti Owners Association International (AOAI) 152

### B
B17 Flying Fortress 84
Bare, Allan 88
Barger, Greg 37
Bauer, B. Patrick 156
Bean, Ashton 62
Bear, Fozzie 106
Beckman, Buzz 96
Beckman, Fran 96
Bendix 48, 67, 68
Boer War 80
Bokon, Lillian 109
Bonnie Doon's 125
Borglum, Gutzon 70, 71
Bourke, Robert 74, 76, 97, 100, 111
Boyer Fire Apparatus Company 56
Brichetto, John 127
Brim, A.E. "Gene" 30
Buehrig, Gordon 74
Burkhart Advertising 56
Bush, George H.W. 71

### C
Carter, Jimmy 71
Century Center 155
Christian, Gladys 136
Chrysler 66, 74, 116, 126
Churchill, Harold 123, 126
Colfax, Schuyler 13
Cornelis, Don 136

### D
Dana, Charlotte 33
Dana, Eugene 33
Dana, Ted 33
Devore, Bob 98
Duplex Phaeton 46
Durbin, F.D. 88

### E
Edison, Thomas 29
Egbert, Sherwood 126, 129, 131
Eisenhower, Dwight D. 107
Elyria, Ohio 30
Ephrata 6
Epworth Hospital 148
Erskine, Albert 36, 42, 53, 62, 81, 149
Erskine Golf Course 149
Everett-Metzger-Flanders 29
Exner, Virgil 74

### F
Fish, Frederick 4, 26, 36
Fleming, Ian 71
Forest G. Hay Funeral Home 11
Frefeld, Germany 6
Frog, Kermit the 106

### G
Gardner, Vince 74
Garford Automobile Company 29, 30
Garland, Judy 70
Gestetner Company 73
Ghia 119
Gilbert, Paul 144
Goodrich, Coy 45
Goodrich, George 45
Granatelli, Andy 135, 157
Grant, Frederick Dent 19
Grant, Robert 107
Grant, Ulysses S. 19
Grundy, Gordon 140

### H
H & C Studebaker 7, 8, 10, 11, 80
Hahn, Rosa 108
Hamilton, Ontario 137
Hansen, Charlotte 110
Hansen, Thomas J. 110
*Harle* 6
Harrison, Benjamin 20
Hauser, M.H. 88
Hay, Mrs. Ralph F. 11
Hayes, Rutherford B. 19
Heaslet, James 36
Hertel, Jim 136
Hodak Motors 100
Hoffman, Paul 118
Holcomb, Phyllis 106
Holcomb, Richard 106
Honeywell 68
Hupmobile 73

### I
Indianapolis 500 53, 58, 59, 60, 107, 129
Izzer buggy 39

### J
J47 engine 88
Jenkins, David Abbot "Ab" 53, 71
JMS Building 148
Joswiak, Trudy 108

### K
Kaiser-Jeep Corporation 89
Kalakua, King 19
Kellogg, Tom 130
Kentucky Wagon Manufacturing Co. 40
Khan, Najeeb 57
King, William Henry 31
Kirkpatrick, Jean 109
Klute, Pat 109
Knoll, Bea 109
Koto, Holden "Bob" 74
Kovatch, Pat 109
Krizman, Andy 122
Kroah, Milton 104

### L
Lafayette 18
Lamberti, Nello 131
Lavanture, Richard 57
Leep, Mike 57
Les Preludes Radiator Mascot 57
Lincoln, Abraham 16
Linkletter, Art 70, 71
Lisbon, Portugal 14
Loewy, Laurence 146
Loewy, Raymond 73, 74, 76, 97, 101, 107, 129, 130, 131, 146
Louis, Joe 70
Lyon Foundation 132, 133, 134

### M
Madrid, Spain 14
Mary-Ann Club 108, 109
Matthews, George 76
McCulloch Corporation 126, 129
McDonnell, Mark 156
Meister, George 29
Memorial Hospital 109
Mercedes-Benz 112
Merrill, Jack 72, 136
Milburn Wagon Company 8, 80
Miller, S. Ray 57, 157
Moore, Audrey 74
Moritz, Virginia 109
Moeser, W.A. 140
Muldoon, Andrew 125
Muldoon, Herman 125

### N
Nance, James 118
Nelson, Byron 71
New Brunswick, New Jersey 88
Newman, Leo 145
Nixon, Bertha M. 108
Norman, Fenton 38
Notre Dame 10, 51, 115, 118, 120

### O
Orange Empire Chapter 106

### P
Packard 115, 118, 119, 120, 123, 125
Palm Springs, California 130
Pasalich, John 88
Pfeiffer, Charlotte 156
Pierce-Arrow 51, 64
Pinetown, Pennsylvania 6
Proving Ground 48, 49, 153

### R
Radecki, Kay 132, 134
Radecki, Ron 132, 134
Reinecker, Warren 112
Reinhart, John 74
Reynolds, Ed 156
Roadster 57
Roberts, Lord 80
Rockne, Knute 51
Rogowski, Dororthy 109
Rooney, Mickey 70
Roosevelt, Eleanor 70
Ruszkowski, Pat 57

### S
Santa Barbara, California 38
Satori, Mira 124
Seidel, William 121
Sexton, Grover 53
Shanghai Horse Bazaar and Automobile Company 45
Sheridan, Philip 19
Sherman, William Tecumseh 19
Sibona-Bassano 132
Slick, Thomas 62
Smucker, Mark 57
Sollitt Construction 95
South Bend Bait Co. 157
South Bend Firefighters Local 362 56
South Bend Lathe 157
South Bend Toy Co. 157
Spence, Nancy 74
Spence, Virginia 74
Spicer, Eli 66, 124
Spicer, Susie 124
Stevens, Brooks 129, 135
Stewart, Joe 38
Studebaker, Bill 92
Studebaker, Carroll 61
Studebaker, Cathy Davis 61
Studebaker, Clement 6, 8, 10, 16, 18, 147, 148, 154
Studebaker, Henry 7, 8
Studebaker, J.M. 8, 10, 13, 18, 26, 27, 28, 34, 148, 149
Studebaker, Jacob 10
Studebaker, John C. 6, 7
Studebaker, John M. 36
Studebaker, John Mohler 7
Studebaker, Peter 6, 10, 15, 39
Studebaker, Rebecca 6
Studebaker, Verneda 61
Studebaker Drivers Club (SDC) 152
Studebaker National Museum 66, 124, 156, 159
Studenbecker, Clement 6
Studenbecker, Henry 6
Studenbecker, Peter 6
Sylvania 134

### T
Teague, Richard 119
Thornton, Joan 110
Thornton, R.W. 110
Tomasso, Victor 47
Toth, Natalie 109
Turin, Italy 132

### U
United Auto Workers 99

### V
Vance, Harold 62, 64, 75
Vassos, George 69
Visible Storage 157

### W
Walkerville, Ontario 139
Weasel 83, 85, 86
Welch, Philip 4, 6
Welch, Sally 4
Welsh, Rosalie 109
Wheelhorse 157
Wilk Brothers 151
Wilson, Woodrow 81
Wood Brothers 16
Wright-Cyclone engine 83, 84

### Y
Yavapai County, Arizona 53
YMCA 149
York, Pennsylvania 6

### Z
Zesinger, Carol 108